Christians are suppo
people; but they still
how should Christians answer this objection, often raised in
evangelistic settings? Dr. Mark Coppenger offers a strategy
for doing so that is biblical, accessible, honest, and seasoned
with wit and wisdom.

THOR MASDEN
Professor of New Testament, Ethics and Philosophy, Midwestern
Theological Seminary, Kansas City, Missouri

This book models concise expression, shrewd logic, clear
organization, subtle wit, brutal honesty, graphic illustration,
cultural savvy, and charitable characterization of opponents.
It answers the title's question as much by showing how
to think about the matter as by seeking out best answers.
Previously I did not know of a great book treating this
question. Now I do. I shall be recommending it to many, as
well as assigning it for student reading – not least because
it so clearly commends the sole means through which the
undeniable Christian 'bad' may find solution.

ROBERT W. YARBROUGH
Professor of New Testament, Covenant Theological Seminary,
St. Louis, Missouri

The bad behavior of Christians is one of the leading objections
raised against the Christian faith. Why are Christians such

hypocrites? Why don't Christians act more like Christ? This is a challenge Christians must address with both clarity and honesty. Mark Coppenger has risen to the task. This book doesn't whitewash the bad behavior of many Christians, but it also offers some helpful insights, theological context, and practical wisdom for how Christians can respond to this important challenge.

SEAN MCDOWELL

Professor of apologetics, Biola University, La Mirada
Author or co-author of more than 18 books including *Evidence that Demands A Verdict*

I know of no one I would rather have tackle the question asked in the title of this book than Mark Coppenger. With his rare mix of broad reading, deep thinking, and practical, 'boots-on-the-ground' work in Christian ministry, Coppenger understands that the question is a loaded one and will never be addressed in a helpful way unless it is first unpacked, carefully considered, and understood. As a result, this book does not avoid real challenges that are legitimately leveled against biblical Christianity. Neither does it offer facile answers that satisfy no one who seriously wants to understand how the way of Jesus Christ can have proponents who sometime spectacularly fail to live up to their professed faith. Coppenger understands the Bible and the nature of real Christianity. Consequently he does not allow false judgments based on misrepresentation to stand. He also understands logical fallacies and effectively—and sometimes humorously—exposes them and contrasts them with legitimate critiques. The result is a book that both answers honest questions about Christians and the Christian faith and serves as an encouragement to any believer who wants to follow Christ more faithfully. So get a copy for anyone who has sincere hesitations about Christianity. Better yet, if you are a Christian get two copies and read it with an honest inquirer. You will help that person consider the gospel of Jesus while strengthening your own faith as you do.

THOMAS ASCOL
Senior Pastor, Grace Baptist Church, Cape Coral, Florida
President, Founders Ministries

Mark Coppenger addresses a key challenge faced by Christians regularly in the increasingly secular societies of the West. He unpacks the detail of the challenge, laying out before readers past examples of Christians who have fallen far short of the requirements of their faith and pointing out how such poor examples of Christianity are grist to the mill of those who would bring the faith to its knees. Coppenger then provides the necessary tools for apologetic responses to the challenge. He provides a brilliant exposé of the fallacy of moral equivalence, showing how it is based on lazy thinking and half-truths. He continues to unveil Christianity's unique internal and external tools for self-correction, pointing to the ultimate answer to the challenge: the life and model of Jesus. Coppenger's excellent written expression results in a highly accessible work that is a must-read for Christians in our sceptical times.

PETER G. RIDDELL

Senior research fellow, Australian College of Theology, Sydney, Australia

THE BIG TEN
Critical Questions Answered

SERIES EDITORS
James N. Anderson and Greg Welty

If Christianity Is So Good, Why Are Christians So Bad?

Mark Coppenger

CHRISTIAN
FOCUS

Copyright © Mark Coppenger 2022

paperback ISBN 978-1-5271-0774-8
ebook ISBN 978-1-5271-0879-0

Published in 2022
by
Christian Focus Publications Ltd,
Geanies House, Fearn, Ross-shire
IV20 1TW, Scotland
www.christianfocus.com

Cover design by Paul Lewis

Printed and bound by
Bell & Bain, Glasgow

CONTENTS

1

Introduction

In what he calls his 'Sortabiography,' Eric Idle devotes a chapter to the making of *Monty Python's Life of Brian*, and he notes a line the filmmakers would not cross:

We agreed early on, you couldn't knock Christ. How can you attack a man who professes peace to all people, speaks out for the meek, heals the poor, and cures the sick? You can't. Comedy's business is some kind of search for truth. Clearly this was a very great man, leaving aside for a minute his potential divinity. No, the problem with Christianity was the followers, who would happily put each other to death at the drop of a dogma. You could be burned alive if you didn't believe Christ was actually in the Communion wafer (what, cannibalism?), and they are still bickering about whether gluten-free bread constitutes the real Christ or not. I mean, it's nuts. Christ admired, saved, and protected women. The followers denied them, locked them up, and insisted in about the twelfth century that the clergy become celibate, with highly predictable results, from popes shagging their daughters to pedophilia.[1]

And so he poses one iteration of the challenge this book takes up: 'If Christianity is so good, why are Christians so bad?' Of course, we Christians face a troubling, much more personal question, 'How can I profess to be a Christian when I myself do so many bad things?' We're more likely to say, 'I'm a sinner saved by grace,' or 'I'm just a beggar telling other beggars where to find food' than, 'Hey, look at me!' Though our focus will be on the general question, we'll touch on the personal as we try to sort this out.

The classic Problem of Evil dwells upon the suffering of innocents in the world, from earthquakes and cancer, to muggers. But a more particular question, a subsidiary inquiry, concerns the unwarranted suffering that comes at the hands of those who profess faith in Christ. It's one thing to be crushed by Hitler, felled by leukemia, or drowned by a tsunami, but how do we account (and how does God justify Himself) for the despicable damage done by professing Christians?

Of course, one could ask the same sort of question of any religious or ideological group. ('If Islam/atheism/Marxism/ Buddhism is so great, why have Muslims/atheists/Marxists/

---

1   Eric Idle, *Always Look on the Bright Side of Life: A Sortabiography* (New York: Crown Archetype, 2018), 99.

Buddhists done so many bad things?') No group should be exempt from such scrutiny. And while some groups stand out as notoriously transgressive (e.g. ISIS), others are shameful for their insularity, for their failure to pitch in when there is great and costly work to do to make the world a better place. Though we'll touch on these matters, we'll leave the corresponding apologetics up to the other parties. We'll let them give an account of the wickedness associated with their faithful.

2

A Few Questions About the Question

Before trying to answer the question, 'If Christianity is so good, why are Christians so bad?,' it's fair to ask a few questions about the question itself.

GENUINE OR RHETORICAL?

First, is it genuine or rhetorical? On the one hand, an inquirer could ask it quite sincerely out of puzzlement. On the other, it could come as a combative challenge, a put down, a reduction to absurdity—something along the lines of 'Take that!' You get this sort of thing in addressing the aforementioned Problem of Evil. On the one hand, a Christian parent who just lost a child might ask with tears, 'How can an all-powerful, all-loving God let this happen?' But from the skeptic, the very same question could come out as a taunt, meant to embarrass the faith of the believer.

We'll address both of these challenges, as well as the anxious who've been challenged, offering a defense of both the faith and the faithful. Within this model, it's an exercise in pastoral encouragement for believers, as well as an effort to push back against the critic's charge – a work of 'apologetics,' if you will. (The word is based on the Greek for verbal/legal defense, *apologia*.) In contemporary English, an apology is more a matter of saying, 'I'm sorry,' of admitting wrong and seeking absolution. To do otherwise is often called 'being defensive,' as if you won't own up to your transgressions. Well, of course, there's a place to acknowledge misdeeds, but there is a difference between 'being defensive' (failing to give the critic a fair hearing) and 'defending what warrants defending' (the purview of apologetics), and I hope we can avoid the first without abandoning the second.

That being said, we should recognize that the behavior of those professing to be Christian can be a source of puzzlement and grief among believers, agnostics and even sympathetic atheists. They really want to know what's going on here. Perhaps unbelievers were counting on better performance by the Church, say, as co-belligerents in a great cause, such as the Civil Rights Movement of the 1960s. Perhaps there are 'seekers' who've just about given up on their skepticism, but aren't so sure they want to ally themselves with a faith group whose track record is suspect. And, of course, there are the Christians who are embarrassed, even mortified, at what they see in Church history, and perhaps within their own congregations. They know, trust and cling to Jesus, their salvation sure, their walk improving as they grow spiritually. But how are they to wrap their minds around the wickedness done by those bearing Jesus' name, and also come to terms with some of the bad things done in Jesus' name? So we will address that as well.

A COMPLEX QUESTION?

Logic teachers speak of 'informal fallacies,' whose use may charm the unwary or sympathetically predisposed, but whose validity is wanting. This isn't to say that their deployment is necessarily and utterly without merit, or that their use proves that the user's claim is false; rather, it might simply mean that the fallacious case is insufficient, that it needs more to make it go. Perhaps the most famous one is *argumentum ad hominem*, attacking the person rather than his or her claim or his or her reasoning, e.g. 'Why should we listen to you? You're just a kid (or an old coot).' Another is *post hoc, ergo propter hoc*, claiming that something that regularly precedes something else must be its cause, e.g. 'All heroin users began on milk. I'm just saying.' Well, there are scores of these so-called fallacies, some with Latin names (e.g. *ad misericordiam,* 'appeal to pity'; *ad baculum,* 'appeal to force'), some with plain old English labels (slippery slope; false dichotomy). Again, application of a fallacy does not kill your cause. You may still be right. But to press your case, you've turned to something that is inadequate (if not downright illicit) but is parading as decisive, and it needs to be questioned. So we cry 'Foul!' and demand something better. Just because you take a cheap shot at a defendant doesn't mean they're innocent. You just need to clean up your act and come at him or her in another way.

The fallacy at issue here in this book is called 'complex question', whereby the query is so loaded as to put the respondent in an impossible fix. For instance, if I ask you, 'Have you stopped beating your wife?' an answer of either 'Yes' or 'No' implies that you have, indeed, beaten your wife. Similarly, the book's question, 'If Christianity is so good, why are Christians so bad?' is loaded. To offer a solution to this mystery implies that you acknowledge that 'Christians are so bad,' so we at least have to consider whether we're being led into a trap.

CRUCIAL DEFINITIONS

It's always fair to ask what someone means by their terms. When, as a Baptist, I'm asked if I'm a Calvinist, I might press them to clarify the concept. Are they asking whether (following John Calvin's reading of the Bible) I believe that Jesus died only for those He had chosen in advance for salvation, or that, once you are saved, you cannot lose your salvation? Or could it be something more, like the practice of baptizing infants or of avoiding visual portrayals of members of the Trinity? Tell me what you mean, and I'll tell you if I fill the bill. Similarly, we should ask, 'How are you using "Christianity" and "Christian"? And what about "good" and "bad"? Furthermore, what makes something *so* good and *so* bad?'

We'll take a look at these terms down the way, but let's note some angles right off. For instance, is someone a Christian if, despite his or her avowals, a court of law couldn't find enough evidence to convict him or her of being one? Also, is Christianity a system of beliefs, a demographic set, a way of life, or essentially a relationship with a person, namely Jesus … or a combination of some or all of these things? And what of the moral and value terms, 'good' and 'bad'? Ethicists of every stamp have struggled with the 'Euthyphro Dilemma' since Socrates pressed it upon a young man around 400 B.C. In that encounter, the philosopher asked, in effect, 'Is something good because God says so, or does God say so because it's good?' In other words, what ultimately defines moral worth and rectitude? What's the basis for declaring something deplorable or admirable, for judging one thing in bounds and another out of bounds?

Then, there's the matter of degree, the presupposition that warrants the use of the modifying word 'so.' Take the case of the lifetime batting average of Ted Williams, who's enshrined in the Baseball Hall of Fame. Someone familiar with the game might marvel, 'What in the world made him so great at the plate, with a cumulative .344 average?' (This means he got a hit that put him on base 344 times out of a 1000.) An outsider might ask, 'How could he be so bad with a bat, failing to reach base with a hit 656 times out of a 1000?' It all depends on realistic expectations. And so it's fair to ask if the critic is utopian, imposing unreasonable standards on a group of people.

To put it another way, what is the 'standard meter bar' they're using to judge goodness? Do they want us to hold a given Christian up to Nelson Mandela for comparison? Immanuel Kant? Mother Teresa? Socrates? Some Platonic Form? Should we go with WWJD ('What Would Jesus Do?') or something more along the lines of WWGD ('What Would Gandhi Do?'), or, in defining badness, WWHD ('What Would Hitler Do?')? Of course, if there were broad agreement over the rightness of genuinely Christian deeds, then this would be a merely academic exercise. But take, for example, the word 'proselytize.' For critics of the faith (and even some who call themselves Christian), it's a dirty word. But for believers following Jesus' 'Great Commission' in Matthew 28:19-20 (to 'make disciples of all nations'), it's a mandate. And just think of the number of instances where Bible quotation from the Gospels and Epistles would be condemned as 'hate speech' on the modern university campus.

It's important to note that Christians are not, themselves, unified on many moral matters, holding their consensus against a hostile world. For we/they disparage one another's pronouncements and behavior on everything from Halloween observance to social drinking to how one votes in presidential elections.

Finally, in this connection, it's fair to ask if the critics are suffering from a form of hypersensitivity (with overweening concern for the slightest slights and inconveniences) or hypochondria (habitually reading grave medical omens into the slightest symptoms).

VARIATIONS ON THE SAME QUESTION

Again, the structure of the question suggests a range of other book titles: 'If atheism (or socialism, Hinduism, agnosticism, academia) is so good, why are atheists (socialists, Hindus, agnostics, academics) so bad?' Or, more charitably, 'If atheism (etc.) is so bad, why are atheists (etc.) so good?' As a group, these questions strike the ear as a bit strange or carelessly assembled. They make sweeping generalizations, perhaps trading in stereotypes, and one wonders if they're going to try to make their case with anecdotes.

Also, we shouldn't limit ourselves to ideologies. What about the question, 'If book publishing is so good, why are books so awful?' or 'If education is so good, why are schools so bad?' Fair is fair.

CALLING THE BRIDE UGLY

Yes, perhaps I'm being fragile and prickly in raising such questions about the question. But in a number of passages, the Bible speaks of the Church as if it were the bride of Christ. (For instance, Ephesians 5:22-24 teaches that wives should submit to their husbands as the Church submits to Jesus.) With that imagery in mind, let me suggest that the lead question of the book, when read as a challenge, implies that the Lord's spouse is ugly. And so I hope you'll indulge me a bit of indignation.

This being said, let's get down to work on particulars.

SUMMARY OF MAIN POINTS

- It's important to begin by taking a close look at the framing of the question itself: 'If Christianity is so good, why are Christians so bad?'
- Some will ask this question rhetorically as a challenge; others will ask it out of genuine puzzlement.
- The question is 'complex' or loaded, in that it contains dubious assumptions.
- Definitions are crucial to clear thinking: in this instance, we need to nail down what is meant by 'Christianity' and 'Christian,' 'good' and 'bad,' ... and even the word 'so.'
- By substituting other groups and institutions (e.g. agnosticism or book publishing) for 'Christianity' in

the central question, we can better judge its tenor and fairness.

3

I Suppose We Asked For It

La Rochefoucauld observed that 'hypocrisy is the compliment that vice pays to virtue.' If you don't recognize high standards, you don't honor them by trying to mask your misbehavior. Or, to put it otherwise, it's hard to be a hypocrite if you don't stand for anything. Christianity stands for a lot and promises a great deal as well, so we're on the spot.

We claim to 'walk in newness of life,' so what's gone wrong with so many professing believers on so many occasions? It won't do to dismiss the bad things done by those calling themselves Christian with a wave of the hand and the fallback, 'We're only human.' Well, yes, we *are* human and not immune to the temptations and delusions that lead men and women into ruinous and hurtful behavior. But we claim that something has happened to us to make us better than we were: a blessing to the world, an example of goodness. Certainly, our Scripture claims as much.

REGENERATION IN THE BIBLE

In Matthew 5:13-16, Jesus says:

> You are the **salt of the earth**. But if the salt loses its saltiness, how can it be made salty again? It is no longer good for anything, except to be thrown out and trampled underfoot. You are the **light of the world**. A town built on a hill cannot be hidden. Neither do people light a lamp and put it under a bowl. Instead, they put it on its stand, and it gives light to everyone in the house. In the same way, let your light shine before others, that they may see your **good deeds** and glorify your Father in heaven.

In other words, believers (as salt) are designed to make culture tasty and to prevent it from rotting. They're meant to show (as light) the way, so that people don't stumble or lose their bearings. Indeed, their performance is to be so excellent that people will come to admire the God whom Christians say they trust.

Jesus continues in John 13:34-35, 'A new command I give you: Love one another. As I have loved you, so you must love one another. By this everyone will know that you are my disciples, if you **love one another**.' When you lay that standard up against the report of a petty church squabble, you have to say that those Christians have some explaining to do.

Then, Paul picks up the theme of radical transformation in 2 Corinthians 5:17: 'Therefore, if anyone is in Christ, the **new creation** has come: The old has gone, the new is here!'

One hears an echo of John 3:7, where Jesus said, 'You should not be surprised at my saying, "You must be **born again**."' That is to say, the Lord makes big changes in a person's life, changes that are marked by conspicuous decency, magnanimity, wisdom, fortitude and grace: blessings to the world.

It's as though we started out as canvas, and He turned us into corduroy, or changed us from poplin to silk. We're made of different stuff once He does His saving work on us. This isn't the sort of thing you hear from other faiths or ideologies. Sure, they say that adherence to a new creed, membership in a new community, and adoption of a new ethos can be revolutionary. On these grounds, Malcolm Little becomes the Nation of Islam's Malcolm X in prison, and becomes the subject of an adulatory film bearing his name as its title and starring Denzel Washington; Ernest Guevara, as a young medical student, is radicalized by the poverty and disease he sees on a motorcycle trip around South America, and he becomes 'Che,' a Marxist revolutionary whose visage is emblazoned on countless T-shirts (and yes, with an adulatory film of his own, *The Motorcycle Diaries*). Big transformations. But if Malcolm and Che had fallen away from their causes, the former reverting to 'Malcolm Little,' the latter re-enrolling in medical school with an eye toward a comfortable practice in Buenos Aires, we wouldn't wax metaphysical. People change. But there's something different going on with Christians, for they are a 'people changed' by an outside, sovereign power, who not only oversees their transformation, but also secures and perfects it. And so, the moral stakes are higher. Christians are supposed to be dramatically and lastingly unique in the world, so much so that consistent departure from the path Jesus set before them even raises questions about the fact of their new birth. Hence, the old slogan I heard in seminary, 'The faith that fizzles before the finale was false from the first.' This puts a cloud over *tu quoque* ('you also') arguments of the form, 'Oh, yeah. Well, you're pretty bad yourself.' That would be like comparing apples to oranges, or, rather, apples to zinc in the spiritual realm.

Picking up again with Scripture, we read that genuine Christians are not just better neighbors; they're more blessed neighbors. As Jesus said in John 10:10b, 'I have come that they may have life, and have it **to the full**.' And sheer force of will cannot explain it. We're not like *The Little Engine That Could*, huffing and puffing up hills, chanting, 'I think I can, I think I can.' Rather, God infuses us with the Holy Spirit, thereby countering our tendency to self-destruct and to torment others. Paul puts it this way in Galatians 5:19-24:

> The **acts of the flesh** are obvious: sexual immorality, impurity and debauchery; idolatry and witchcraft; hatred, discord, jealousy, fits of rage, selfish ambition, dissensions, factions and envy; drunkenness, orgies, and the like. I warn you, as I did before, that those who live like this will not inherit the kingdom of God. But the **fruit of the Spirit** is love, joy, peace, forbearance, kindness, goodness, faithfulness, gentleness and self-control. Against such things there is no law. Those who belong to Christ Jesus have crucified the flesh with its passions and desires.

The first set sounds like program notes for an afternoon tabloid talk show. The second collection sounds wonderful, the sort of list that would make one ask how those professing to be followers of Christ could be so objectionable and miserable.

DOCTRINAL STATEMENTS ON THE NEW LIFE

Through the millennia, Christians have insisted in their doctrinal statements—confessions and creeds—that believers enjoy, a moral upgrade. For instance, the *Anglican Articles of Religion* (XI) says that good works, while not sufficient for salvation, 'are the fruits of Faith ... and do spring out necessarily of a true and lively Faith; insomuch that by them a lively Faith may be as evidently known as a tree discerned by the fruit.' Similarly, Article XVI in the **Roman Catholic Decrees of Trent** says that 'Christ Jesus Himself, as the head into the members and the vine into the branches, continually infuses strength into those justified, which strength always precedes, accompanies and follows their good works ...'

The **Abstract of Principles (1859)**, a founding document for the Southern Baptist Convention's oldest seminary, reads, 'Regeneration is a change of heart, wrought by the Holy Spirit, who quickeneth the dead in trespasses and sins enlightening their minds spiritually and savingly to understand the Word of God, and renewing their whole nature, so that they love and practice holiness.' The **Canons of the Synod of Dort (1619),** speak of the efficacy of the 'regenerating Spirit,' which 'pervades the inmost recesses of the man ... opens the closed and softens the hardened heart ... infuses new qualities into the will, which, though heretofore dead, he quickens; from being evil, disobedient and refractory, he renders it good, obedient and pliable; actuates and strengthens it, that, like a good tree, it may bring forth the fruits of good actions.' And so, on it goes: as the day follows the night, so too does ethical nobility issue from the Spirit's saving activity.

Biblical Examples

One of the glories of the Bible is that it is so full of instructive examples, concrete instances that demonstrate the ideals:

Mark 5:1-20 tells the story of a mad man, the **Gadarene demoniac,** who ran naked through the graveyards and cut himself until he met Jesus, who freed the man of tormenting, debilitating demons. The result was dramatic and unnerving: 'When they came to Jesus, they saw the man who had been possessed by the legion of demons, sitting there, dressed and in his right mind; and they were afraid.' (5:15).

Also in the Gospels, we read of another transformative example in Luke 19:1-10, which recounts the salvation of **Zacchaeus,** who went from being a dishonest tax collector to a conscience-stricken man who resolved to repay fourfold anything he took unjustly. And then, in Acts 9, we read of **Paul** (born Saul), transformed from a murderous persecutor of Christians to an evangelist who suffered for the gospel and ultimately gave up his life for the faith.

EXAMPLES FROM CHURCH HISTORY

Not surprisingly, there are countless biographies tracking such transformation. **Augustine** is a classic case in point. In *Confessions*, he describes his sordid early life. He'd fathered a child out of wedlock, and, in his youth, he'd stolen apples with some friends—not to enjoy the eating, but just for the thrill of transgression. In this vein, I recently came across a Catholic course called 'Saints with a Past,' which encouraged students not to despair over what evil they might have done. Just look at those whose beginnings were anything but promising: St. Callixtus (an embezzler and brawler); St. Mary of Egypt (a seductress); St. Moses the Black (a cut-throat and gang leader); St. Olga (a vengeful mass murderer); St. Vladimir (guilty of fratricide and polygamy); St. Margaret of Cortona (a rich man's mistress); and St. Camillus (a mercenary and card shark).[1]

In Protestant circles, one can point to a wide range of cases, including the classic, eighteenth-century transformation of **John Newton**, who had been a captain of slave ships. Following his encounter with God, he'd become an Anglican priest, zealous for the abolition of slavery, best known today as author of the confessional hymn, 'Amazing Grace.' In it, he describes his former self as a blind 'wretch,' lacking the fear of God, but then testifies to the Lord's kindness and mercy in giving him spiritual sight and strength for the journey through this frightful world and on to heaven.

Moving on to the twentieth century, we come to **Nicky Cruz**, the New York City gang leader who came to Christ through the ministry of David Wilkerson, the founder of Times Square Church. (The story is told in *The Cross and the Switchblade*.) Leaving the comfort of his church in the Pennsylvania countryside, Wilkerson traveled to the streets of New York to preach the gospel, reaching out to gangs,

---

1   Thomas Craughwell, *Saints with a Past: A Study of Conversion in the Lives of Eight Notorious Sinners,* Audio CD – Unabridged (Catholic Courses, 2011).

such as the Mau Maus. When, eventually, he rented a hall for a substantial preaching event, he asked the gangs to attend and then to take up the offering.

At the altar call, as Cruz recounts, 'I was the first one at the rail. I kneeled down and said the first prayer of my life and this was it: "Dear God, I'm the dirtiest sinner in New York. I don't think You want me. If You do want me, You can have me. As bad as I was before, I want to be that good for Jesus."' [2]

More recently, Laura Hillenbrand's recounting of the life of **Louis Zamperini** (*Unbroken: A World War II Story of Survival, Resilience, and Redemption*) has generated two movies. One (*Unbroken*) focused on his endurance as a prisoner of war under the Japanese in World War II; the other homed in on his spiritual turnaround through faith in Christ (*Unbroken: Path to Redemption*).

An Olympic runner in the 1936 Olympics, Zamperini had gone on to serve as a B-24 bombardier in the Pacific, where his plane crashed and he managed to survive forty-seven days adrift in a life raft before being hauled in by the Japanese. His athletic notoriety made him the special target of a vicious camp guard, Sgt. Mitsuhiro Watanabe, nicknamed 'The Bird.' At war's end, Zamperini seemed to be doing well, with a new wife and speaking opportunities

---

2   David Wilkerson, with John and Elizabeth Sherrill, *The Cross and the Switchblade*, (Old Tappan, NJ: Spire/Fleming H. Revell), 91

as a hero. But he couldn't shake his memory of Watanabe's brutality; it haunted his dreams and he thought of returning to Japan to find and murder him. He turned to alcohol to medicate his torment, and he was beginning to lose his family when his wife persuaded him to attend a 1949 Billy Graham crusade ... and it was there that he turned in faith to Jesus.

The nightmares stopped. He poured his alcohol down the drain, and he lost his taste for vengeance. In 1952, he traveled to Japan, where he had the opportunity to speak of the gospel to imprisoned war criminals. At the close, he asked officials for the chance to meet with the very guards who'd abused him:

> I looked out and saw them coming down the aisle and, of course, I recognized each one of them vividly. I didn't even think of my reaction—I jumped off the stage, ran down and threw my arms around them, and they withdrew from me. They couldn't understand the forgiveness. We went in the room and there, of course, I continued to press the issue of Christianity, you see. And all but one made a decision for Christ.[3]

As for that reluctant one, he couldn't understand how such forgiveness was possible:

---

3   Louis S. Zamperini, *Olympian Oral History*, Interview with George A. Hodak (Los Angeles: LA84 Foundation, 1988), 89. Accessed October 20, 2021, at https://reasonabletheology.org/the-rest-of-the-story-louis-zamperini-after-unbroken/.

I said, 'Well, Mr. Sasaki, the greatest story of forgiveness the world's ever known was the Cross. When Christ was crucified He said, "Forgive them Father, they know not what they do."' And I said, 'It is only through the Cross that I can come back here and say this, but I do forgive you.' Then he responded to the invitation to become a Christian.

The accounts from Church history go on and on, as chronicled in Kerr and Mulder's *Conversions: The Christian Experience*.[4] In 1651, a poor repairman and a veteran of Oliver Cromwell's army named **John Bunyan** entered upon his Christian pilgrimage having had, by his own account, 'few equals … both for cursing, swearing, lying, and blaspheming the holy name of God.' He became a preacher, for which he was imprisoned. There, he penned an account of his conversion, *Grace Abounding to the Chief of Sinners*, and the allegorical *Pilgrim's Progress*, the most widely read book of English literature other than the Bible until the twentieth century.

Frontier Methodist preacher, **Peter Cartwright**, hailed from a Kentucky county nicknamed 'Rogue's Harbor.' He saw one brother hanged for murder and a sister slide into degradation. He himself was fond of drinking and gambling, and he showed little or no promise as a man until

---

4   *Conversions: The Christian Experience*, edited by Hugh T. Kerr and John M. Mulder (Grand Rapids: Eerdmans, 1983).

one evening in 1801, he was struck with shame and regret over the dissipation of his own life and he began to seek the Lord with fear and trembling, retreating to a cave for prayer. Converted under the preaching of a Presbyterian, James McGready, he began, in 1803, over eight decades of ministry. Known as 'God's Breaking-Plow,' he brought a fervent conversionist and revivalist message to rough elements of the American wilderness and took a strong anti-slavery stand in the years before the Civil War.

Major League Baseball player **Billy Sunday** was sitting drunk on a curb in Chicago in 1886 when he heard a band playing with an invitation to the Pacific Garden Mission. He answered the call, heard the preaching, accepted Christ as his Savior and Lord, and eventually entered into a life of gospel ministry and social action, including support for women's suffrage, opposition to child labor, and inclusion of black people in his meetings, at a time when they would ordinarily have been banned.

ORDINARY SAINTS ON THE SPOT

Well, of course, every cause has its 'spiritual athletes,' moral heroes that the great mass of believers can cheer from the bleachers (or, rather, from the pews). One might argue that it would be folly to expect much from these spectators in various states of unfitness. Besides, the fine talk of the creeds presents ideals or honorific definitions, rather than reliable descriptions of the workaday Christian.

But the Bible won't let us get away with that, for the Apostle Paul speaks indiscriminately of church members in exalted terms. Notice, for example, his opening salutation in Philippians 1:1: 'Paul and Timothy, servants of Christ Jesus, To all God's **holy people** in Christ Jesus at Philippi, together with the overseers and deacons.' Indeed, in many translations of this verse, he calls them '**saints**.' Following today's common parlance, you might think that all super Christians (aka, 'holy people' and 'saints') would have been set apart as bishops and deacons, but here Paul uses the expression for the rank and file. These weren't the folks who would one day be given special honors on the church calendar, not a John Chrysostom (whose 'golden mouthed' preaching championed the poor in fourth-century Constantinople), or a William Tyndale (the sixteenth-century scholar who, despite strong opposition, translated the Bible into English), or a William Wilberforce (whose efforts as a member of Parliament led to the abolition of the British slave trade in 1807). Just regular 'guys and gals' doing their Christian thing as best they could under challenging circumstances.

So it won't do to say, 'Okay, I made a mess of things, but what do you expect? I'm not a saint.' Alas, none of us Christian nobodies is off the hook.

The problem is, we've set a high standard (or rather had a high standard set for us), so it's no wonder that we're called into account.

SUMMARY OF MAIN POINTS

- You have to stand for something to qualify as a hypocrite. Christians do, indeed, stand for exalted things, so it is fair to hold them accountable for their behavior.
- The Bible says that being 'born again' means that a major transformation has occurred in the soul of the new believer and that the difference between a Christian's previous and current life should be obvious. This dramatic transformation is reflected in the faith statements of various denominations and is illustrated by the conversion accounts of people in the Bible and throughout Church history.
- Ordinary Christians, and not just heroes of the faith, are answerable to a supernatural standard.

4

Some You Might Have Missed

C ritics round up the 'usual suspects,' such as leaders and other participants in the Crusades, the Inquisition, the Wars of Religion, witch trials, and the brutalities of imperialistic colonialism. They play this as a trump card, meant to neutralize Christian claims of unique goodness; indeed, of goodness at all. Of course, there are some valid responses to some of these charges, but that can wait for later. For the moment, let's own up to the problems and mention some folks the gainsayers probably missed.

'TOXIC CHRISTIANITY' WITHIN MY EXPERIENCE

I should start by saying that my own performance as a Christian has been toxic on many occasions. Reflecting on misdeeds in my childhood (I was saved at age seven), in my youth, and as recently as yesterday, I have things to regret and confess to the Lord. So when I talk of poisonous personalities and deeds you might have missed, I acknowledge my own sins (though I'll spare you, or more likely myself, the details). I'm not writing from a lofty, 'Aren't *they* awful?' standpoint. With that understanding, let's take a look outward.

In my own life, I think back to the early 1960s, to the mistreatment of a Nigerian Baptist leader who decided to come to America to further his education at a Baptist college, which was connected to the missionaries with whom he'd worked back home. The problem came when he sought to join our big Baptist church within an easy walk from the campus. You'd think that people who'd been singing, 'Red and yellow, black and white, all are precious in His sight' all those years would welcome him with open arms, but, when the big day came for the congregational vote, hundreds marked their ballots against him. Happy to report, many more affirmed his application for membership, and he was, indeed, added to the church roll, but the nastiness of the event is vivid in my memory almost sixty years later.

This was the Jim Crow era in the segregated South, and many of our people were convinced that 'he would be happier with his own people' at a black church on the west end of town. Not surprisingly, the day of the vote, a bunch of members not normally seen in church showed up, and we had to bring in chairs to seat folks in the aisles. The atmosphere was tense and acrimonious, and the motion to go with a secret ballot instead of a hand vote passed easily.

Of course, a lot of what was going on wasn't so secret, for we knew very well that our Sunday School teacher (who'd commented on the upcoming vote) was against it, as was the teacher of the 'old men's class' (who spoke against it in the service) and the wealthy woman who'd just bought us new choir robes (and who left the church in a huff). It was hard to process; it still is.

Then there was my Wheaton colleague who spoke of the terror he experienced as a pastor's child, when his father's annual call came around in the church. He knew the vote was impending, and he'd be distracted at school, worrying that the family would be out on its ear in the weeks ahead and that the town, including his classmates, would know his dad had been rejected. I'm sure the church felt that this was a reasonable fire-break against incompetence or malfeasance in their leadership, a way to handle things without having to make a big fuss. But it didn't count the psychic impact on the minister's family, the way it left them dangling and fearful, rather than cherished.

In that same time frame, I heard of a pastor's family who'd been cast out because a prying member, perhaps a deacon or elder on a maintenance visit, was looking through their closets in the parsonage, where he discovered a dress with a pricey label in it (one from Nieman-Marcus, as I recall). He didn't know that the dress was a gift from a relative and not a sign of personal extravagance. For one thing, it was none of his business. For another, it wasn't a disqualifying issue. For yet another, if he'd had the decency to ask, he could have gotten his story straight. Sad to say, the family got a good deal of grief from this judgmental invasion of privacy.

Later, in seminary, I heard the story of another 'detective,' this time in a little Texas church. As the story goes, a busybody was looking through the young pastor's library while he was off for class at the seminary. He discovered a copy of the Revised Standard Version, which translated the Isaiah passage referring to Mary as 'young woman' instead of 'virgin' (Isa. 7:14). Concluding that the mere possession of a copy of this version was tantamount to flirting with denial of the virgin birth, or giving aid and comfort to the publisher who printed such trash, the censor boxed up his books and put them in the hall. When the student got back to the church, he discovered this graphic portrayal of his termination, as if he were an adulterous husband who came home to find his clothes thrown out on the lawn.

A FEW TROUBLING EXAMPLES FROM CHURCH HISTORY

History books of every sort recount the misdeeds of 'Christian' villains, many of them familiar to critics of the faith. We're reminded repeatedly of the tyranny of the inquisitor, Torquemada; the grotesque 'ministry' of Rasputin; Ulrich Zwingli's order to drown Anabaptist Felix Manz in Zurich's Limmat River; the execution of heretic Michael Servetus in John Calvin's Geneva. And, of course, in recent decades, we're continually exposed to the sexual escapades or worldly extravagances of high-visibility ministers, well-publicized embarrassments to chasten and humble Christians. Who hasn't heard of the dalliances of Jim Bakker and Jimmy Swaggart, or the mind-boggling appeal of Jesse Duplantis for funds to purchase a $50 million jet because the three already in his fleet were too small to permit non-stop flights to some locales?

The press makes sure we're well aware of these embarrassments. But there are always other 'gems' to mine, wherever one might dig. Here are a few that even seasoned critics might have missed:

Clifton S. Carnes: In August, 1928, Southern Baptists learned that Clifton Carnes, the treasurer of their Home Mission Board, had embezzled nearly one million dollars (over fourteen million in today's dollars) and fled to Canada, where he was apprehended and returned to Atlanta. In short order, he was convicted and consigned to federal prison for five years. Historians speak of it as the 'Carnes Defalcation.'

Carnes's rise to (much-abused) power began when an outside accounting firm sent him to the board for a routine audit. The trustees (particularly the businessmen) were so impressed with his work that they brought him on as bookkeeper, and, in 1919, elevated him, with church endorsements, to the position of treasurer. None suspected that he had a criminal past and that his employment at the firm was facilitated by the shortage of men during World War I.

The next year, Southern Baptists launched a massive fundraising effort, the '75 Million Campaign,' and early results were dazzling. Flush with bounty, the Board virtually doubled their budget and expenditures in a single year, but then gifts slowed as the country was hit with the Depression of 1920–1921, with staggering deflation and a 37 per cent drop in wholesale prices, the largest since the end of the Revolutionary War. Vastly overextended, the board gave Carnes *carte blanche* to arrange loans and apply the funds as he saw fit to address the debt. And thus, unencumbered by accountability, he misappropriated money to his own advantage.

In the end, the convention paid off the debts and the board's ministry was rescued, but not before Southern Baptists were reminded that just because one bore the title of Christian, there was no guarantee that they were immune to fiduciary negligence or outright felony.

Samir Geagea: Lebanon, now the home of the terrorist group, Hezbollah, has been torn by strife, not only between Muslims and Christians, but also between Christian sects. A case in point was the struggle between rival 'Christian' militias, who had split over Trinitarian matters centuries earlier. One of the groups, the Maronites, traced their existence back to a fourth-century hermit named Maron, and Samir

Geagea, current President of the Lebanese Forces, a Lebanese Christian-based political party and former militia, was one of his spiritual progeny. Driven by both political goals (favoring ethnic districts over a unified Lebanon) and a hundred-year-old blood feud with a rival village, he teamed up with another Maronite, Bashir Gemayel, to attack yet a third Maronite, Tony Franjieh. It's complicated, but Theodore Dalrymple did his best to sort it out, historically and morally:

> On 13 June 1978 Geagea amassed a thousand of his Phalange [from the Greek *phalanx*, for 'battalion'] troops at Jounieh and drove up into the mountains at night. Another force of around two hundred came down from Bsharre. In all around 1,200 Phalangists were involved, all heavily armed with machine guns, cannons and rockets, moving in two convoys of open-topped jeeps.
>
> The diversionary force from Bsharre attacked first, just before four a.m., ambushing and killing the militia men woken by the first sounds of battle. This drew the defenders away from the centre of Ehden, leaving the Franjiehs' Summer Palace undefended. And it was on the Summer Palace, where Tony Franjieh lay sleeping, that Geagea directed the main Phalangist force. He led it into battle himself ... By the time the raiders withdrew, Tony Franjieh and his entire immediate family had been killed.
>
> I pointed out to Ch'baat that rousing a man from his bed and killing him and his family in their pyjamas

hardly seemed [honorable] ... but he simply shrugged his shoulders. 'Geagea is a very honourable and very holy man,' he said. 'We are very proud of him in Bsharre.'

I listed some more of the crimes I had heard Geagea accused of: as well as the killing of Tony Franjieh, the equally cowardly night murder of another Christian rival, Dany Chamoun and his wife and two small sons (twenty-seven bullets were pumped into the two children); the bombing of the church in Jounieh (apparently an attempt either to keep the Pope away or to persuade the international community that the Christians of Lebanon were being oppressed and terrorised by wicked Muslim extremists); the mass murder and terrorising of the Druze of the Chouf.

'You must not believe what people say about Samir Geagea,' said Ch'baat.

'But you can hardly call him holy.'

'Certainly yes,' he said, quite serious. 'He went to mass every day and prayed by his bed every night. He had a church built wherever he was, wherever he fought. Every Christmas his troops expected money as a present, but instead he gave them prayer books and rosaries. Of course, he went to confession every week. He never went into battle without his cross. In his office, he always had a picture of the Virgin and a cross: never any picture of Che Guevara or anything like that.'[1]

Thomas Hobbes, Sr: The English philosopher, Thomas Hobbes (Jr), is best known for his work of political philosophy, *Leviathan*, the one where he described the state of nature as 'solitary, poor, nasty, brutish, and short.' Against this horrific backdrop, where every man had a right to take every other man's property and life, men surrendered their personal rights to the government, which would bring and preserve order. Hobbes would have no patience with subsequent Jeffersonian (and Lockean) talk of our being 'endowed by our creator with certain unalienable rights,' which, according to the U.S. Declaration of Independence, legitimate governments must honor.

Hobbes's work is materialistic and indifferent, if not hostile, to the Church, and perhaps we should look to his father for influence. In his fascinating book, *Faith of the Fatherless: The Psychology of Atheism*, New York University psychology professor Paul Vitz speaks of the elder Hobbes:

> [He] was the vicar of a small Anglican church outside London. There was little to admire about him. He is described as ignorant, of a choleric temper, and given to cardplaying; apparently, he sometimes fell asleep

---

1   William Dalrymple, *From the Holy Mountain: A Journey in the Shadow of Byzantium* (London: Flamingo/HarperCollins, 1997), 253-255.

during the services over which he presided. When another parson provoked him at the church door, there was a fight in which the elder Hobbes struck his opponent, after which he fled beyond London. His family never saw or heard from him again, and he died in obscurity.[2]

Though Hobbes Jr disclaimed atheism (perhaps as a matter of prudence in seventeenth-century England), his work was thoroughly materialistic and hostile to both Church and traditional Christianity. He did, indeed, introduce the notion of a social contract, so much in play today, but his baleful take on natural man 'in a war of all against all' did not lead him to commend a separation of powers; rather, sovereign power must control every sector of society, Church and speech included.

Benjamin Collins McGehee: In my high school years, I had occasion to spend a number of days lodging and dining in Little Rock hotels: the Marion, the Lafayette and the Grady Manning, thanks to participation in the All-State Band. By Arkansas standards, these buildings were grand affairs. For instance, the Marion, in whose ballroom we rehearsed, was the tallest building in the state when it was constructed in 1907, and through the years, until its destruction in 1980,

2   Paul C. Vitz, *Faith of the Fatherless: The Psychology of Atheism* (Dallas: Spence, 1999), 34.

it boasted such visitors as Eleanor Roosevelt, Harry Truman, Douglas MacArthur, Will Rogers and Helen Keller.

The Grady Manning was originally the Benjamin McGehee, built in 1930 by Benjamin Collins McGehee, a man descended from Highland Scots who took firm root among the Methodists in the South. His mother was raised in a Methodist minister's home, and, when Ben's father died, he and his siblings donated memorial windows to a Methodist Church. By all accounts, he was an upright man. So why list him as problematic? Because he operated a segregated hotel in the 'Jim Crow' era. I've talked about racial sin within my childhood church, but here, it spilled out of the church into the marketplace. Though the establishment likely hired African-Americans as cooks and maids, neither these employees nor their families could reserve a room for a stay.

What's the evidence? As I turn through the 1963–1964 edition of *The Negro Travelers' Green Book*, I find none of these hotels to be welcoming to black travelers. I see the Graysonia on Gaines, the Honeycut, Miller, and Tucker's on West 9th, the Charmaine on West 14th, and Mrs. H. Gilmore's Tourist Home on West 19th.[3] The shortlist of available properties leaves out a host of lodging options for these people, even excluding veterans who had fought in

3   *The Negro Travelers' Green Book: Guide for Travel and Vacations* (New York: Victor H. Green & Company, 1959), 9.

World War II and Korea. (President Truman had integrated the armed forces in 1948; before that, they had served in such fabled units as the Tuskegee Airmen and the 761st Tank Battalion.)

These Little Rock hotels were genteel and professional. No police dogs roamed the corridors. No firehoses were trained on 'troublemakers' at the entrance. They were places of polite talk and monitored manners. But they were party to an astonishingly unjust system, as were countless hotels throughout the city, many of which had faithful churchgoers in management, Benjamin Collins McGehee included. After all, this was the American 'Bible Belt.' But the *Green Book* extends its embarrassing listings throughout the land, from Maine to California. Yes, there were signs of progress. The Ben Franklin Hotel in Philadelphia, which turned away the Brooklyn Dodgers in 1947 (the year Jackie Robinson, as a Dodger, broke the color barrier in Major League Baseball) shows up as a welcoming venue in the 1959 *Green Book*. But it took the Civil Rights Act of 1964 to force a lot of Christian people to act Christianly in this matter by offering public accommodation to people of all races and ethnicities.

It might seem churlish to add Brother McGehee, an active Methodist, to the same list as Carnes and Geagea. I have no reason to think he wasn't a genuine Christian. For all I know, he might have been willing to risk his life to pull a black person from a burning car, or perhaps he contributed to one of the historic black colleges, such as Grambling or Fisk. I simply use him as a token of the baleful practice in place throughout the land, one enabled, if not enforced, by saints in the pews. Maybe I should have put the onus on lifelong Episcopalian, Eleanor Roosevelt, who supported the Tuskegee Airmen by taking a flight with one of their pilots and who later spearheaded the effort to frame the Universal Declaration of Human Rights. But, when she visited Little Rock, she didn't insist on patronizing one of the city's *Green Book* hotels or restaurants, going, instead, to a Jim Crow establishment. There was plenty of complicity to go around.

LITIGATION

Though the New Testament urged Christians not to go to court against each other, the halls of justice are all too acquainted with ecclesiastical grievances—some valid, some not—hashed out before the bar. A journal devoted to the latest in litigation, *Church Law and Tax Report*, provides depressing but important reading in this connection. Indeed, the cases that surface as cautionary tales do not paint a pretty picture.

A single issue (September/October 2017) recounts the story of a Muslim convert who asked that his transformation be kept confidential. However, the church posted footage of his baptism, and now he claims that he suffered serious abuse for it when he returned to the Middle East. Another case concerned an organist who vandalized his church by spray painting inflammatory words on the wall, hoping to stir up political feelings against a newly-elected American president, addressing him with 'Heil' and adding a 'gay slur and a swastika.' He wanted it to pass as 'hate speech' from outside vandals, but he was in fact the one who did the deed.

Then, there was a church given a million-dollar bequest: half of it designated for general operation and maintenance, the other half assigned for upkeep of its cemetery. The problem was the church had recently sold the cemetery, so the pastor, with a background in financial management, said they should take only half of the money, since the purpose for the second half was a nullity. Nevertheless, the church trustees would have none of this and acted to fire him.

Of course, there's plenty of blame to pass around. The deplorable pastor phenomenon didn't begin or end with Thomas Hobbes's father in the sixteenth century. In *Churches That Abuse*, contemporary sociologist and cult-watcher, Ronald Enroth, details the cruelties of groups with a control-fanatic in charge. In one congregation, members were required to report one another's faults to the pastor; another pastor staged congregational all-nighters, where groups undertook 'public verbal executions,' with sins charged face to face in front of the body; another discouraged departures to attend a parent's funeral: 'Let the dead bury the dead.' There were also those who were taught that they should forego insurance, glasses and medical care for their kids, since it would show a lack of faith in God's physical provision.

Instances of 'church discipline,' where the unfortunate behavior of a member triggers dismissal, can generate some serious conflict. Some of these cast-outs drag the churches into court, charging zealous overreach in shaming them— as if the congregation bombed the city to rubble and then bombed the rubble to make it bounce.

And so on it goes. Just type 'toxic Christianity' into any search engine and you'll find plenty of blogs decrying despicable players and ploys. Of course, you'll also find that some of the complainers, themselves professing Christians, act despicably, getting even 'in print' with decent people who hurt their feelings by doing decent things. So yes, there is plenty to complain about. The grim taxonomy features a range of unfortunate species, whether hateful zealot, treacherous gossip, or conniving shyster.

IT CAN HURT TO LAUGH

Comedian Emo Philips has a classic routine that plays off the way that Christians can fall into vicious stupidity, or stupid viciousness:

> Once I saw this guy on a bridge about to jump. I said, 'Don't do it!' He said, 'Nobody loves me.' I said, 'God loves you. Do you believe in God?'

He said, 'Yes.' I said, 'Are you a Christian or a Jew?' He said, 'A Christian.' I said, 'Me, too! Protestant or Catholic?' He said, 'Protestant.' I said, 'Me, too! What franchise?' He said, 'Baptist.' I said, 'Me, too! Northern Baptist or Southern Baptist?' He said, 'Northern Baptist.' I said, 'Me, too! Northern Conservative Baptist or Northern Liberal Baptist?'

He said, 'Northern Conservative Baptist.' I said, 'Me, too! Northern Conservative Baptist Great Lakes Region, or Northern Conservative Baptist Eastern Region?' He said, 'Northern Conservative Baptist Great Lakes Region.' I said, 'Me, too!'

'Northern Conservative Baptist Great Lakes Region Council of 1879, or Northern Conservative Baptist Great Lakes Region Council of 1912?' He said, 'Northern Conservative Baptist Great Lakes Region Council of 1912.' I said, 'Die, heretic!' And I pushed him over.[4]

SUMMARY OF MAIN POINTS

- A Christian need not look beyond his/her own life or the life of his/her congregation to find disappointing behavior by those calling themselves disciples of Christ. Personal and local illustrations abound.

- Should critics of the faith run out of notorious examples, we can supply others to embarrass the Church. And, indeed, Christian misbehavior can invite biting parody.

---

4   Emo Philips, 'The best God joke ever—and it's mine!' *The Guardian* (September 29, 2005). Accessed June 25, 2018, at https://www.theguardian.com/stage/2005/sep/29/comedy.religion.

5

The Bible Tells Me So

Though the Bible promises great transformations and fruitfulness for the people of God, it also offers a stern reality check, one that explains the failings of the redeemed.

WORKS IN PROGRESS

While Scripture teaches that a fundamental change occurs in the life of the new believer as he or she is 'born again' or regenerated, he or she is not yet completely wonderful, but is rather a work in progress.

This is not to say that the convert's behavior is lackluster, compared to what it will be in a few years. Often, the first days following conversion are marked with holy zeal. Some new believers are able to step away, instantly and forever, from crippling addiction. Others are eager to evangelize, to share their faith with all who will listen. Still others begin to treat their families with radically new grace, so that the household is amazed and relieved at the same time. But the wear and tear of life can scrub off some of the luster, and old challenges can reawaken old, worldly habits of mind. Disappointments can prompt the return of worry; jolts can resurrect old expletives we thought we'd laid to rest; irritating colleagues or neighbors can sap our joy and sense of God's providence; old temptations rear their heads when we're tired. And so we can slip a bit. (The old joke is that the brand-new Christian was so excited and effectual as servant and representative of the Lord that he or she had to backslide to have fellowship with the veterans in the congregation.)

Nevertheless, there is a *telos* (an ultimate aim) to our Christian lives, one toward which the Lord steers us. As Paul told the Christians in Philippi in the opening words of his letter to them, he was confident that God would complete the good work He had started in them 'until the day of Jesus Christ' (Phil. 1:6, KJV). Yes, he knew from first-hand experience that there would be spiritual struggles and temporary reversals, the sort of conflict he rehearsed in a famous passage in Romans 7: 'I have the desire to do what is good, but I cannot carry it out. For I do not do the good I want to do, but the evil I do not want to do—this I keep on doing' (Romans 7:18-19). So even the great Apostle, who wrote a sizeable portion of the New Testament, was no stranger to internal strife.

BORN AGAIN; NOT FAST-FORWARDED TO SPLENDOR

When Jesus told Nicodemus in John 3 that he must be 'born again,' He didn't say he had the opportunity to be fast-forwarded to splendor. There was no promise that, should regeneration occur, he would find himself a fully mature and winsome being. That's not the way birth works. Newborns are a mess, socially inept, unselfconsciously selfish and addled babies.

Indeed, Paul speaks of baby Christians in 1 Corinthians 3:1-3:

> Brothers and sisters, I could not address you as people who live by the Spirit but as people who are still worldly—mere infants in Christ. I gave you milk, not solid food, for you were not yet ready for it. Indeed, you are still not ready. You are still worldly. For since there is jealousy and quarreling among you, are you not worldly? Are you not acting like mere humans?

And he highlights another facet of infancy in 1 Corinthians 13:9-12, an epistemological feature that helps account for stumbling:

> For we know in part and we prophesy in part, but when completeness comes, what is in part disappears. When I was a child, I talked like a child, I thought like a child, I reasoned like a child. When I became a man, I put the ways of childhood behind me. For now we see only a reflection as in a mirror; then we shall see

face to face. Now I know in part; then I shall know fully, even as I am fully known.

PARABLES

In three of the Gospels (Matthew, Mark and Luke), Jesus gave the Parable of the Sower (or Soils) to explain the way in which some professions of faith are only temporary. As Jesus explains, sometimes the gospel does, indeed, take root and spring up in a person's life, with a show of green, but the soil is shallow, and the roots can't sustain growth. Though the start was promising, disappointment soon follows, as the seedling withers in the sun. There are also plants that manage to take off with a fine display of vitality, but are eventually choked off by encircling weeds. Again, nice start, temporary encouragement: eventual ruin.

And so it is in our churches today: decisions for Christ marked with tears, increased church attendance, a more circumspect lifestyle and even a willingness to commend the faith to others. But something happens and we lose track of them. As one observer of my denomination put it, 'Millions of members and the FBI can't find half of them.'

NEEDFUL EXHORTATIONS

You'd think that the Apostle Peter would have his act together. After all, he'd been tutored face to face by Jesus during His pre-crucifixion years and then cleansingly humiliated by the post-crucifixion Jesus for his empty bragging and subsequent betrayal during Passion Week. Yes, he'd seen the ingathering of Gentiles at Pentecost and would prove to be faithful unto a martyr's death. And though he was no stranger to nervous bluster, he would one day be anointed to write stirring epistles for our New Testament. But, as Paul showed in Galatians 2:11-21 (a few decades before Peter wrote his two New Testament letters), Peter could become befuddled and 'fold like a cheap suit' under peer pressure:

> When Cephas came to Antioch, I opposed him to his face, because he stood condemned. For before certain men came from James, he used to eat with the Gentiles. But when they arrived, he began to draw back and separate himself from the Gentiles because he was afraid of those who belonged to the circumcision group. The other Jews joined him in his hypocrisy, so that by their hypocrisy even Barnabas was led astray (Gal. 2:11-13).

If Peter could blow it, then so could the rest of the people 'in the pews'; hence, the Apostles' many rebukes, exhortations and instructions for the congregants to step up their game. Paul's letters are famous for their closing pleas, things that needed to be said because the readers and hearers were far from perfect. For instance, he wraps up his message to the Colossians with calls to give up sexual immorality, impurity, lust, evil desires, greed, anger, rage, malice, slander, filthy language, surliness within the family, second-rate service in the workplace and unfairness.

Just imagine a parent dropping his freshman off at college and saying such things right before the budding student got out of the car and headed to the dorm. You can hear him saying, 'Come on, Dad! What do you think I am? That's insulting!' But Paul would not be deterred, because he knew the sorts of baggage these former 'pagans' were carrying. And they knew that he knew, but also that he loved them.

More uplifting, but equally convicting, were the positive admonitions, that, for instance, the Colossians should exhibit compassion, kindness, humility, gentleness, patience, love, forgiveness, mutuality, edification, respect, diligence, prayer, wisdom and graceful conversation. Again, if these were already their conspicuous characteristics, Paul would have had no reason to emphasize them.

His exhortations were not meant as an exercise in browbeating the Christians into being something unthinkably wonderful. It wasn't like whipping a dog to get him to do algebra; rather, disciples have supernatural power available to them.

Earlier, we read 2 Corinthians 5:17: 'Therefore, if anyone is in Christ, the new creation has come: The old has gone, the new is here!' But we also find, in Ephesians 4:22-24, that the old has a way of sticking around, and that it's a problem that needs attention:

> You were taught, with regard to your former way of
> life, to put off your old self, which is being corrupted
> by its deceitful desires; to be made new in the attitude
> of your minds; and to put on the new self, created to
> be like God in true righteousness and holiness.

So it's a both-and situation, whereby we have a new self, with some nagging old ways. In my preaching, I sometimes illustrate the situation by means of 'grave wrappings.' I bring out several strips of linen a few feet long and ask the congregation to imagine that I'm Lazarus, a few days after being delivered from the tomb. Once the initial excitement has passed, I, Lazarus, have begun to get annoyed with a range of things: sand flies, an irritating nephew, disappointing food, a thankless boss. So I begin to fantasize about going back down into the tomb where it was cool and quiet. As I talk, I begin wrapping my arm with cloth.

I then imagine the search for me, one that takes friends back into the tomb, only to find me laid out in wrappings. When they ask me what I'm doing, I recount my complaints and the comforts of the grave, only to hear back, 'Okay. We get it. But there's one big problem. You're alive, not dead! You look ridiculous. Get out of those rags and get back up into the world.'

Of course, there is much better preaching on the matter. In an 1855 sermon on Romans 15:13, 'The Power of the Holy Spirit,' the great British pastor, Charles Spurgeon, spoke of his difficulty in dealing with a wayward imagination. Though it sometimes took him up to 'the gates of pearl,' it also took him down to 'the vilest kennels and sewers of earth.' This was an outworking of the fact that 'presently corruption still resides even in the hearts of the regenerate. At present the heart is partially impure. At present there are still lusts and evil thoughts.' He then reflected, 'Can you chain your imagination? No; but the power of the Holy Ghost can.'

BIBLICAL 'CHARACTERS' INDEED

'Father Abraham' lied to Pharaoh to save his own skin, and was rebuked by a 'pagan' for doing this; David, a 'man after God's own heart,' was guilty of adultery and murder; Peter, 'The Rock,' ran for cover at Jesus' moment of greatest peril, even denying his association with the Lord. These, and other examples, show that the biblical writers were not hagiographers in the rose-colored-glasses mode; they were candid in identifying sub-Christian 'parishioners,' who dishonored the Fellowship. Here are a few:

Judas: Of course, he's a strong case in point. He was one of The Twelve, a member of the inner circle, who traveled with Jesus, observed His miracles, sat under His anointed teaching, and endured some hardship along the way. But he proved to be a grasping traitor, willing to betray Jesus to His enemies for thirty pieces of silver.

Diotrephes: In 3 John, the Apostle John labeled him as one who loved to be a big shot, who slandered John and other church leaders, and who even expelled fellow congregants who wanted to welcome saintly visitors. He was a bone-headed, treacherous bully, crippling the church. And who knows what damage he'd done before John put a stop to his reign of ecclesiastical terror?

Euodia and Syntyche: In Philippians 4:2, the Apostle Paul urged these two women to 'be of the same mindset as Christ Jesus'; in other words, to quit their bickering. Apparently, their rivalry had become an existential threat to the fellowship, and he singled them out for rebuke. It's also reasonable to surmise that they had jointly taken unchristian positions on an issue; otherwise, he would have simply told one of them to stop it. Some commentators suggest that the great passage commending Christlike humility and sacrifice (Phil. 2:5-11) was directed both at them and at those who were cheering on the sidelines for one contestant or other in their ungodly fight.

Demas: He's one of the saddest characters to be found in Scripture. He shows up as one of Paul's trusted colleagues in both Philemon and Colossians. But then, in Paul's last letter, when his time is short as a captive on 'death row' in Rome, he asks Timothy to come to him, since, as he puts it, 'Demas, because he loved this world, has deserted me ...' (2 Tim. 4:10). Thus, one of 'the faithful' bails out on Paul in his time of maximum vulnerability. It's not clear what it was about this 'present world' that Demas loved: perhaps the safety of anonymous or marginal connection with Christ; perhaps better income and creature comforts; or perhaps a reversal of lifestyle to one of 'wine, women, and song.' We can only guess ...

He was on board before he wasn't, and so it is with many who identify with Jesus, only to betray Him. Not surprisingly, the world is not particularly scrupulous at distinguishing departed Demases from faithful church members, so we may find ourselves charged unfairly with their 'Christian' offenses.

Ananias and Sapphira: In Acts 5, Paul confronted this married couple who'd lied to him and the church. They'd made a production of selling a plot of land and then saying the proceeds went to the Lord's work, even though they'd kept some back. When confronted with the fact, they dropped dead, either from God-permitted heart attacks or from God's direct killing blow. Of course, any number of church members have lied without losing their lives, but, as the story makes clear, it's a grave offense.

Simon the Sorcerer: In Acts 8, we learn he was highly regarded by the people in the town, renowned for his perceived power, which they attributed to God. But he came to hear Philip, was taken by the message and believed it, was subsequently baptized, and then followed the Apostle around, observing his miracles. Then, things went wrong. Those were the days when God was demonstrating the astonishing truth that 'even Gentiles' could be saved, and He was vouchsafing this truth by dramatic manifestations of the Holy Spirit, such as speaking in tongues at the point of their conversion. When word came to Peter and John that some were responsive to the gospel up in Samaria, they went to these people, laid their hands upon them, and invoked the Spirit.

This electrified Simon and he offered money to get the same thing, which was a big mistake. Peter, who was not afraid to speak his mind, turned on him for thinking God's economy was tied to human financial strategies, and he dismissed Simon in the strongest possible terms, essentially writing him out of the kingdom. He urged him to repent, and we hope he did. But not before his creepy offer gave birth to a new word: the sin of 'simony.'

In *The Divine Comedy*, Dante Alighieri consigns simonists, the 'offspring' of Simon Magus, to the eighth ring of hell, the ninth being the bottom, where Lucifer is cast. These are the people who think that spiritual and ecclesiastical favors can be traded for 'silver and gold,' scoundrels who sought to tie spiritual things to money. Thus we read in Canto XIX:

> O Simon, Magus, and O you wretched crowd
> Of those who follow him and prostitute
> In your rapacity the things of God.

> Which should be brides of righteousness, to get
> Silver and gold—it is time the trumpet sounded
> For you: the third pouch [of ten in hell's eighth ring]
> is where you are put.[1]

A DISAPPOINTING ROLL CALL OF CHURCHES

In Chapters 2 and 3 of Revelation, the Lord indicts a number of His churches, though He acknowledges their good points on the way to criticism. He grants that they've been through the wringers of persecution and poverty and have stuck together as churches. They've done a lot of good things along the way, but there are big problems:

- Ephesus has 'forsaken the love' it had in the beginning.
- Pergamum has indulged some who cling to dangerously false teachings.
- Thyatira has tolerated a corrupting, deluding 'Jezebel' in their midst.
- Sardis is spiritually dead.
- Laodicea is smugly materialistic and spiritually lukewarm.

Only Smyrna and Philadelphia escape a warning.

These people didn't live in the 'Bible Belt,' but had, rather, been tried in the fire and found faithful in many, if not all, respects. Nevertheless, infection had set in. As we put it in

---

1   *The Inferno of Dante: A New Verse Translation*, Robert Pinsky (Farrar, Straus and Giroux, 1994), 151.

contemporary terms, for some of these congregations, 'the world had gotten into the church more than the church into the world.'

REFLECTED IN CREEDS

The Bible and experience teach that those who identify as Christians are not always exemplary. As the Lutheran *Augsburg Confession* observes in Article VIII, 'in this life many false Christians, hypocrites, and even open sinners remain among the godly.'

In Question 35 of the *Westminster Shorter Catechism*, we read that believers are on a developmental journey, whereupon they become more blameless, more saintly or sanctified:

> Q. What is sanctification?
> A. Sanctification is the world of God's free grace, whereby we are renewed in the whole man after the image of God, and are enabled more and more to die unto sin, and live unto righteousness.

Notice that it says, 'enabled more and more to die unto sin,' not 'enabled instantaneously and completely to die unto sin.' It's a process, and, wherever you take a sampling from a person's life short of heaven, you will find faults.

In *A Catechism for Boys and Girls* (1798), Richard Cecil picks up on this teaching:

97.Q. Is this process of sanctification ever complete in this life?
A. No. It is certain and continual, but complete only in heaven ...

98.Q. What hinders the completion of sanctification in this life?
A. The Scripture says 'The flesh lusts against the Spirit so that you cannot do the things you would.'

In *A Catechism of Bible Teaching* (1892), John Broadus writes, under 'Lesson 10: Justification and Sanctification':

8. Is sanctification complete at once?
A. No, sanctification is gradual, and ought to go on increasing till the end of the earthly life ...

So, yes, the Bible (and sermons and creeds built upon it) teaches that Christians have been and will be, individually and collectively, guilty of sins, while, at the same time, marked by intimations of splendor. It's going to be a mixed bag till the end of history.

SUMMARY OF MAIN POINTS

• Scripture covers the sad spectacle of believers performing in sub-standard ways: for one thing, being 'born again' does not mean being 'born spiritually into full maturity.' Otherwise, the Apostles would not have urged those they recognized as genuine Christians, including Peter, to clean up their behavior.

- Sometimes, the Apostles would reprimand individual believers, such as Euodia and Syntyche; other times, they would criticize churches, such as Ephesus and Laodicea.
- In some instances, new disciples prove to be misfires, with Judas being the most notorious case. The Parable of the Sower speaks to this phenomenon.
- Under the category of 'sanctification' (the convert's gradual progress in Christlikeness), doctrinal and instructional documents of the Church address the believer's uneven journey toward spiritual perfection, a journey which will be completed only in the afterlife.

6

Are You Sure About That?
The Problem of False Professors

The expression, 'false professor,' doesn't refer to a university scholar/teacher who landed the job on the strength of forged reference letters and a phony curriculum vitae, claiming degrees he or she never earned. Rather, it denotes those who profess allegiance to Jesus Christ as Savior and Lord yet are not, in reality, subjects of His kingdom. Note the modifier 'false,' as distinct from 'mendacious.' The 'false professor' is probably not lying, but is speaking sincerely, convinced that he or she is, indeed, bound for heaven. They go to church, deploy biblical expressions, and keep their nose clean, more or less. Believing that God 'grades on the curve,' they find themselves in the middle of the pack of those professing the same faith they declare, and above the average score of the general populace. Demographers count them as Christian, and they are generally recognized as such in the community, even within their own family. But the matter is not settled.

THE 'NO *TRUE* SCOTSMAN' FALLACY

Ah, but am I trying to finesse my way out of difficulties? The crusading atheist, Antony Flew, who later turned theist, impressed with the Argument from Design, thought so. He identified what's now called the 'No *True* Scotsman' fallacy — arbitrary stipulation meant to insulate broad claims from counterexamples (as in 'No *true* Scotsman would put sugar in his porridge'; and then there's an American version, 'No true Chicagoan puts ketchup on his hot dog'). Another crusading atheist, Christopher Hitchens (who did not come around to theism before his death), wielded it against those who might try to defend the honor of their religion by expelling subscribers who didn't act honorably. Here, he applies it to Buddhists:

> 'Buddhism has a lot to teach us, you know. It's been shown to have real psychological and cognitive value.'

> 'You mean like those Buddhist monks who helped the Burmese army ethnically cleanse the Rohingya to the point of genocide?'

> 'Oh, but they weren't proper Buddhists.'[1]

---

1 Christopher Hitchens, Richard Dawkins, Sam Harris and Daniel Dennett, *The Four Horsemen: The Conversation That Sparked An Atheist Revolution* (New York: Random House, 2019), xi.

But, of course, this is too easy. Understand, though, that not-really-an-x claims are sometimes right. Though Louis Farrakhan may say he leads the Nation of Islam, it's fair to observe that his group, like Grape Nuts (neither grape nor nuts), is neither a nation nor Islamic. (Malcolm X and Warith Deen Mohammed made the same observation as they departed Elijah Mohammed's fold.) The question, then, is one of essentials, of necessary-and-sufficient criteria.

Groups do, in fact, spell out their essentials. Muslims call theirs 'Pillars'; Protestants speak of 'Solas' (or 'exclusives,' such as 'Faith Alone'). Some Christians perform doctrinal 'triage,' ranking first, second and third order commitments. Evangelicals have identified four distinctives:

- Conversionism: the belief that lives need to be transformed through a 'born-again' experience and a lifelong process of following Jesus.
- Activism: the expression and demonstration of the gospel in missionary and social reform efforts.
- Biblicism: a high regard for and obedience to the Bible as the ultimate authority.
- Crucicentrism: a stress on the sacrifice of Jesus Christ on the cross as making possible the redemption of humanity.

These four criteria were arguably crucial in the minds of the Apostles and other leaders of the Early Church. They're not arbitrary and biblically unsustainable—unlike such judgments as 'No true Christian would work in Caesar's household' or 'No true Christian would fail to memorize at least fifty psalms.' But it's fair to say, 'No true Christian would say that Jesus was an exemplary, yet ordinary, man, whom God adopted for His purposes' or 'No true Christian would remain a willful criminal throughout his life.' The first is a matter of heresy, the latter of inconsistency with regeneration or declarations of the Lordship of Christ. And so we may ask, legitimately, 'Are you sure that the bad Christian you reference is a Christian at all?' (It's the same sort of fairness we would show in the challenge, 'You say you're a true Muslim, but you have steadfastly refused to perform the pilgrimage to Mecca, despite having the funds to do so.' We're not talking about arbitrary, customary incidentals.)

CULTS

A common distinction in Christian theology is between a 'sect' and a 'cult.' The first more or less holds to the ancient creeds of the Church, e.g. Nicene and Apostolic, and builds their doctrine from Scripture. Of course, there are disagreements at the borders, as when Protestants and Catholics are inclined to count each other as sects, construing one another as denominations either scrubbed of important traditions or encrusted by unimportant or deleterious ones. So they may wrangle over whether a hierarchy—'rule by priests'—or, rather, 'the priesthood of all believers' is warranted. But they still will join in reciting the Apostles' Creed, with particular agreement on the doctrine of Christ. Not so, the cults.

In September of 1857, members of a Mormon militia in Utah (some disguised as Indians) attacked a wagon train bound for California, killing 120, including women and older children. This act of territorial frenzy is known as the Mountain Meadows Massacre, its perpetrators members of the Church of Jesus Christ of Latter-day Saints, but it's hard to find the true Christ in their faith. Though the Mormons tip their hats to the Bible (the King James Version), they maintain that it's corrupted, and so they must rely upon the nineteenth-century revelation of Joseph Smith through the *Book of Mormon*, *The Pearl of Great Price*, and *The Doctrine and the Covenants*. They paint a very different picture of Jesus, construing Him as a brother of Lucifer and our forerunner in divinity. The curious story goes on, with proxy baptism for the dead, a four-story afterlife, beginning at the bottom with outer darkness (where Satan and the 'sons of Perdition' are consigned), and ascending through telestial, terrestrial, and celestial realms. So, if critics try to lay the guilt of the Mountain Meadows Massacre (or the creepy behavior of polygamists; or the denial of 'the priesthood' to black people well into the 1970s) on Christianity, they misfire. Of course, Mormons claim to be Christians, but this is wishful thinking on their part. (Of course, this doesn't mean that they aren't typically upright or admirable—just that their uprightness and admirability are not grounded genuinely in the Bible.)

The same goes for Christian Science, a creation of Mary Baker Eddy, whose *Science and Health with Key to the Scriptures* presents a quasi-Eastern religion, with this world being something like a veil of Maya, an illusion that we must penetrate to get to the salubrious otherworld. (Again, with the Grape Nuts, Christian Science is neither Christian nor scientific.) According to their model, sickness is an illusion, which should be addressed by spiritual 'practitioners' rather than genuine physicians. So, when one reads that a boy has died of some malady or another because Christian Science parents didn't bother to take him to the emergency room, it is utterly unfair to lay guilt at the feet of Christianity.

Of course, particularly egregious examples of this sort of false advertizing arose in Nazi Germany, with its 'German Christian Movement,' '*Völkisch* Christianity,' 'German Evangelical Movement,' 'German Faith Movement,' and 'Positive Christianity.'

'Lord, Lord'

The Mormons and Christian Scientists go off the rails on theology, but there's another way to go off the rails: by behaving so outrageously that one's performance makes a mockery of one's profession as a follower of Christ. In Matthew 7:21-23, Jesus said,

> Not everyone who says to me, 'Lord, Lord,' will enter the kingdom of heaven, but only the one who does the will of my Father who is in heaven. Many will say to me on that day, 'Lord, Lord, did we not prophesy in your name and in your name drive out demons and in your name perform many miracles?' Then I will tell them plainly, 'I never knew you. Away from me, you evildoers!'

In the same chapter, Jesus declares that 'wide is the gate and broad is the road that leads to destruction, and many enter through it. But small is the gate and narrow the road that leads to life, and only a few find it' (verses 13-14). So, when we argue that 'no true Christian' would do certain terrible things—such 'unchristian things'—we are not engaging in sleight of hand, but rather tracking with the teachings of Jesus. Indeed, non-Christians are heard to challenge us on these very grounds: for instance, 'I thought you said you were a Christian, but that wasn't a very Christian way to act, defrauding your neighbor' (or 'punching the man who insulted you' or 'slandering your teacher' or 'sleeping with your neighbor's wife').

It's bad enough if it happens once in a moment of weakness, but if it fits a willful pattern, it's hard for one to sustain a claim of personal salvation. It's one thing to tell a lie and then repent; it's quite another to lie chronically—to be a *liar* in one's nature—for that would seem to belie a profession of new birth in Christ.

Let's consider a notorious case in point: the staggering reports of sexual abuse, particularly pedophilia, implicating Roman Catholic priests. Take, for instance, a Pennsylvania grand jury report dealing with six of the eight dioceses in the state (covering fifty-four out of sixty-seven counties, with Philadelphia and Altoona-Johnstown having already been investigated).[2] The jury heard testimony from dozens of witnesses, subpoenaed and reviewed half a million pages of internal diocesan documents, and found 'credible allegations against over three hundred predator priests,' with over a thousand victims, most of them boys, some of them pre-pubescent. They estimated that the real number ran into the thousands, but that the Church had covered things up and destroyed records. They concluded that all the complaints were brushed aside, in every part of the state, by church leaders who preferred to protect the abusers and their institution above all.

---

2 Fortieth Statewide Investigating Grand Jury, REPORT-I, Interim—Redacted. Accessed November 4, 2018, at https://www.courthousenews.com/wp-content/uploads/2018/08/pa-abuse-report.pdf

The report runs to over 450 pages and details elements of abuse and cover-up, naming names, dozens of them, and providing documentation. In the former group, one priest, a teacher, would take early-teen girls on trips in his car, remove his collar and ask that they not call him 'Father' as he violated them; another lured victims to jobs in the rectory with ready supplies of video games, soft drinks and candy, and assured them that he was acting as 'an instrument of God' as he drew them into sordid activities. These abusive priests' ingenuity was prodigious, with one helping a boy learn 'how to check for cancer' and another telling altar boys to wear nothing under their cassocks since God didn't want 'man-made' clothes worn next to their skin while serving mass. It goes on and on for hundreds of pages, and this is for only a section of Pennsylvania.

As for the cover-up, the grand jury listed categories of diversion and deception: the use of euphemisms such as 'inappropriate contact' and 'boundary issues,' instead of 'rape'; the employment of lame investigatory techniques by fellow clergy or by church-run psychiatric offices, who relied largely on each priest's 'self-report'; keeping everything in-house, with the parishioners and police in the dark; continuing to provide housing and living expenses despite the credibility of the charges. And, in their case studies, they detailed the careers of the priests, as they were moved from place to place, but not dismissed or defrocked. They might be put on 'sick leave,' given a 'leave of absence,' or reassigned to a rehabilitation house because of 'burn out' from teaching, or put in charge of the charity clothing drive.

So the question is not only whether the abusing priests were 'saved,' but also whether those sheltering the abusers were 'saved'? Of course, a hardy critic could say I'm just trotting out the 'No True Scotsman' device, but surely the burden of proof has shifted to the party who insists that these priests were *bona fide* followers of Christ. Whatever they may say, we must answer to 1 John 2:4: 'Whoever says, "I know him," but does not do what he commands is a liar, and the truth is not in that person.' Clearly, the Bible teaches that sex with minors is contrary to God's commands regarding sexual purity; ignore that counsel, and you forfeit your Christian-disciple card. Though the world may insist that the Church is stuck with these serial abusers, the Church is perfectly free to expel them on principle, a practice we'll address in Chapter 8.

THE IGNORANCE FACTOR

That being said, a mitigating word is due regarding the Body of Christ. As a budding pastor, I made enough mistakes of my own, but I think there were occasional times when my congregational critics were wrong. I'd followed a long-tenured pastor who didn't share my enthusiasm for biblical inerrancy, and I was convinced that he'd spun things in some unfortunate directions. It was easy for me to get in a huff or a funk over the spiritual recalcitrance of the parishioners, but I was humbled and helped by a little slogan I posted above my study desk. It read, 'Don't attribute to malice what can be explained in terms of ignorance and confusion.'

C.S. Lewis provides an illustration of this principle in his book *Mere Christianity* when he observes that the Salem witch trials were based not upon hatred of people who practiced a different religion, but rather upon the mistaken notion that these were people with supernatural powers and the will to wreak mortal havoc on good folks. Lewis writes:

> One man said to me, 'Three hundred years ago people in England were putting witches to death. Was that what you call the Rule of Human Nature or Right Conduct?' But surely the reason we do not execute witches is that we do not believe there are such things. If we did—if we really thought that there were people going about who had sold themselves to the devil and received supernatural power from him in return and were using those powers to kill their neighbours or drive them mad or bring bad weather, surely we would all agree that if anyone deserved the death penalty, then these filthy quislings did. There is no difference of moral principle here: the difference is about matter of fact.[3]

---

3   C.S. Lewis, *Mere Christianity* (New York: Touchstone, 1996), 26.

The witch-hunters were wrong, as everyone now recognizes, but they weren't parochially malevolent.

WELL-INTENTIONED DRAGONS

An apt title for good-hearted people who do objectionable things, is 'well-intentioned dragons,' the title of a book by Marshall Shelley.[4] These are people who, with honorable motivations, still grieve pastors and cripple churches, making them a spectacle before a watching world. Shelley provides a working taxonomy, featuring *The Bird Dog*, who 'loves to be the pastor's eyes, ears and nose, sniffing out items for attention'; *The Wet Blanket*, who has 'a negative disposition that's contagious'; *Captain Bluster*, who 'comes from the union steward school of diplomacy and speaks with an exclamation instead of a period'; *The Fickle Financier*, who 'uses money to register approval or disapproval of church decisions'; *The Busybody*, who 'enjoys telling others how to do their jobs'; *The Sniper*, who 'voids face-to-face conflict but takes pot shots in private conversation'; *The Bookkeeper*, who 'keeps written record of everything the pastor does that "isn't in the spirit of Christ"'; The *Merchant of Muck*, who 'breeds dissatisfaction by attracting others who know he's more than willing to listen to, and elaborate on, things that are wrong in the church'; *The Legalist*, whose 'list of

---

4   Marshall Shelley, *Well-Intentioned Dragons: Ministering to Problem People in the Church* (Waco: Word/Christianity Today, 1985).

absolutes stretches from the kind of car a pastor can drive to the number of verses in a hymn that must be sung.' (To be fair, one could also make a convicting list of pastoral foibles that retard the work of the church.)

Of course, some of these people are lost, Christians in name only—'tares among the wheat'—but some are just Christian works in progress, exhibiting more or less helpful or hurtful personality traits as they are progressively sanctified. You might say it's a matter of trajectory, as suggested in this catechetical item from John Broadus (*A Catechism of Bible Teaching* [1892], 'Lesson 10: Justification and Sanctification'):

> Q. What is the sure proof of being a true believer?
> A. The only sure proof of being a true believer is growing in holiness and in usefulness, even to the end. (2 Pet. 1:10)

In other words, he or she is headed in the right direction, despite less than awesome performance in the present and regrettable setbacks along the way. Furthermore, God can use a range of personality types in His body. Indeed, you might be able to find Peter in the 'Captain Bluster' role now and then, and perhaps it was a 'Busybody' who, by telling on the misbehavior of Euodia and Syntyche, prompted Paul to write the luminescent passage on Jesus in Philippians 2:5-11.

So yes, there are some genuinely unpleasant, 'high maintenance' Christians, and we may claim them as part of the tribe. But we have very good reason to object to some of the lumping-together that our critics employ. In this connection, I hope that we might be excused for revisiting Misters Geagea and Carnes in Chapter 3, and ask that skeptics might forgive us if we suggested they were 'no true Scotsmen.'

SUMMARY OF MAIN POINTS

- It's fair to ask if the offender in question is really a Christian; Jesus Himself speaks of phonies who call Him 'Lord' but are not in His fold.
- Some groups bear the name 'Christian,' but are manifestly not so.
- Though it can be suspiciously convenient to disqualify embarrassing or appalling churchmen out of hand (reserving the label 'Christian' for those you want to claim as members of the body), there is a time to do so legitimately.
- The local church features an interesting garden of difficult types: some members don't yet know better; others may suspect that they're out of line, and are slowly coming around to full realization and reformation. Addressing these matters is a messy but holy enterprise.

7

Are You Sure About That?
Doubtful Narratives

I n the opening pages of Genesis, Satan deliberately
misconstrues the Lord in tempting Eve, telling her that
God commanded her not to eat of a certain tree in the
Garden of Eden since He 'knows that when you eat from it
your eyes will be opened, and you will be like God, knowing
good and evil' (Gen. 3:5). I heard one pastor say that this
was both a New Age conceit and the oldest lie. Of course,
there was an element of truth in this, as there is in many
lies: she would indeed become acquainted with a whole new
world of evil in the Fall, and, since God Himself knew the
horrifying prospects, in that respect the first couple would
have a bit more commonality with Him. But she had no
idea what she and Adam were getting into. Instead of 'being
like God' in the ways she imagined (with great wisdom and

power), they would find themselves more ungodly and less capable.

Satan is called the 'Father of Lies' and he uses a variety of media to spin things unfairly against Christians. As said above, we have plenty to be embarrassed, even ashamed, about, but it's worthwhile to question some of what's said about us.

THE ENTERTAINMENT INDUSTRY

An attorney friend recently told me how television shows centering on forensic medicine were terribly misleading, making the work of prosecutors absurdly difficult. Saturated with the entertainment industry's portrayal of open-and-shut cases, solved neatly in an hour or so on the basis of a partial fingerprint, a carpet fiber, a DNA trace, or a phone record, jurors have come to expect exotic yet tidy demonstrations of guilt or innocence. Problem is, the evidence is typically much sketchier and the analyses less reliable than the popular shows suggest.

Similarly, the populace can get a very skewed notion of the Church and ministry from the captains of 'Hollywood' and their counterparts throughout the world. For one thing, ministers, and explicitly Christian laymen, are largely absent from the scene. It's hard to say whether the producers, directors, and writers are wary of, baffled by, or hostile toward portrayals of religion. Whatever the case, a good many in the entertainment industry seem to follow the lead of Prime Minister Tony Blair's public relations adviser in saying, 'We don't do God.' (This problem first struck me after I viewed Steven Spielberg's film, *E.T.*, where none of the characters involved showed the slightest interest in or knowledge of the deliverances of Church and the Bible.) The sum effect is to suggest to the public that, if protagonists don't need God, then we don't either. He's not even a useful fiction, and He and His people will probably just get in the way.

When the church does show up, the ministers are often feckless. I think of the countless screen funerals I've seen where awful people are laid to rest under the exalted and reassuring words of some pastor or priest, as if the Way were immeasurably broad. And then there are the tiny homilies, sounding more like something on a Starbuck's cup than an exposition of the Word. When these clergy are cast into field situations, they're more likely to coo or dither or wring their hands than walk in the footsteps of a prophet, apostle, or elder. Again, ministers seem more a waste of office than an agent of the Lord Almighty. The producers seem to be saying, 'If only they'd do something really helpful, like organize grievance groups in tough neighborhoods, search for a cancer cure, or fight against global warming.' They may appear lovable, as in the case of Father Mulcahy in *M*A*S*H*, but there's no way that fellows like this are capable of the heavy lifting needed for the really big undertakings.

But this is not enough. The industry seems hellbent (literally) on putting God's people in a bad light, with scoundrels appearing way out of proportion to their actual occurrence in the Church. I think immediately of the murderous psychopath played by Robert DeNiro in *Cape Fear*, with Bible verses tattooed all over his body. Other examples come easily to mind, but one might start with a list featured on the Internet Movie Database (imdb.com) under the heading, 'Movies that Mock, Twist, and Slander Scripture, God, and Christianity.'

With so much help from the entertainment media, it's no wonder that people get the general impression that devout Christians are pathetic, creepy, or malevolent—either not part of the solution or actually part of the problem.

THE PRESS

For a season, I worked in the communications office of our denomination, and I had almost daily contact with religion editors at the nation's newspapers and press services. We also subscribed to a clipping service, bringing us dozens of stories each week. While much of what we read was reasonable, there was a preponderance of dissatisfaction over our determination to insist on allegiance to biblical inerrancy in our schools and agencies. And many journalists and columnists were frustrated by our stand against the abortion industry and our resistance to the normalization of homosexuality. One thing I noticed was their eagerness to use the expression, 'religious right,' while scarcely ever speaking of the 'religious left.' It finally struck me that 'right' and 'left' meant 'right of me' and 'left of me.'

I was also irked by the way many of them called the 'conservative resurgence' party 'fundamentalists,' while labeling their opponents 'moderates.' It seemed to me that they were applying the harsh word to the first and the pleasant to the second. It would be better, I thought, to either go harsh with both ('fundamentalist' and 'liberal') or nice with both ('conservative' and 'moderate'). I ventured to suggest this to the religion editor at Associated Press, and I was able to bolster my case with an entry from the *Associated Press Stylebook*:

> **fundamentalist:** The word gained usage in an early 20th century fundamentalist-modernist controversy within Protestantism. In recent years, however, fundamentalist has to a large extent taken on pejorative connotations except when applied to groups that stress strict, literal interpretations of Scripture and separation from other Christians.
>
> In general, do not use fundamentalist unless a group applies the word to itself.[1]

---

1   *The Associated Press Stylebook and Briefing on Media Law 2017,* edited by Paula Froke, Anna Jo Bratton, Oskar Garcia, David Minthorn, Karl Ritter, and Jerry Schwartz (New York: Basic, 2017), 390.

Happy to report, he made the change graciously. (And in another context, several of us were able to persuade some Catholic leaders that there was a difference between 'fundamentalists' and 'evangelicals.')

THE PERILS OF HAGIOGRAPHY AND 'HAGIOCLASM'

Extravagant hagiographies were once mainstays in Christian literature. The word itself simply means 'lives of the saints,' biographies of inspirational figures in Church history. And it has been extended to cover glowing, relentlessly positive accounts of secular figures. Of course, the point is edification, and the reader is not necessarily misled by the author's leaving out embarrassing material. It's assumed the subject is human, with foibles, so we may proceed with the uplifting material. But arguably, a more well-rounded picture of the subject would add to the salutary effect since it would help us identify with the hero or heroine as we ourselves seek a higher path.

The big problem arises when the hagiography trades on moral perfection or fantastical legends to drive home its point, that here is a figure to be venerated. For instance, the Irish monk, St. Fursey, is described thus:

> [H]e was comely to look upon, chaste of body, earnest in mind, affable of speech, gracious of presence, abounding in wisdom, a model of abstemiousness, steadfast in resolution, firm in right judgments, unwearied in longanimity, of sturdiest patience, gentle

in humility, solicitous in charity, while wisdom in him so enhanced the radiance of all the virtues that his conversation, according to the Apostle, was always seasoned with wit in the grace of God.[2]

And then there are the marvelous deeds attached to St. Benedict. It is said that a young boy from the monastery went to the lake to draw water, but fell in, and the current carried him 'a stone's throw' away from shore. No problem:

> Though inside the monastery at the time, the man of God was instantly aware of what had happened and called out to Maurus: 'Hurry, Brother Maurus!' ... What followed was remarkable indeed, and unheard of since the time of Peter the apostle! Maurus asked for the blessing and on receiving it hurried out to fulfil his abbot's command. He kept on running even over the water till he reached the place where Placid was drifting along helplessly. Pulling him up by the hair, Maurus rushed back to shore, still under the impression that he was on dry land.[3]

So yes, some Christian writers seriously overdo it when bragging on exemplary believers. But the practice of

---

2   Pere H. Delehaye, *The Legend of the Saints: An Introduction to Hagiography*, transl. by V. M. Crawford (London: Notre Dame/ Longmans, Green, 1961), 25.

3   Odo John Zimmerman, transl. *St. Gregory the Great: Dialogues* (New York: Fathers of the Church, Inc., 1959) in *Medieval Saints: A Reader*, edited by Mary-Ann Stouck (Peterborough, Ontario, Canada: 1999), 179.

defaming 'saints' is quite widespread as well, and just as misleading. Such writing goes out of its way to denigrate a respected figure by not only highlighting the weaknesses and missteps, but also by ignoring or discounting the strengths and admirable achievements. Love may be blind, leading one to overlook flaws, but the opposite is true: contempt can stupefy you. When this occurs, we fall into what I'll call 'hagioclasm.' 'Hagiography' is writing meant to justify sainthood designation. Substitute 'clasm' for 'graphy' and you speak of wrecking a purported saint's reputation. (It's an echo of 'iconoclasm,' referring typically to the destruction of images in the form of paintings and statuary in a church.)

Christopher Hitchens excoriated Mother Teresa (herself the object of hagiography and expedited beatification), with a book *The Missionary Position*, whose snarky, gratuitously-sexual title signaled a hit job. And, not surprisingly, he's even had a hard word to say for the Quakers. In a dialogue with other famous atheists, he submitted this judgment:

> HITCHENS: And I agree that I'm not likely to have my throat cut at the supermarket by a Quaker. But the Quakers do say, 'We preach non-resistance to evil.' That's as wicked a position as you could possibly have.
>
> HARRIS: Given the right context, yes.
>
> DENNETT: Yes, they're free riders.

HITCHENS: Yes. Read Franklin on what the Quakers were like at the crucial moment, in Philadelphia, when there had to be a battle over freedom, and see why people despised them. I would have said that Quakerism was actually quite a serious danger to the United States. So, it's a matter of space and time ….[4]

Similarly cranky was Lytton Strachey, of the Bloomsbury Group, whose *Eminent Victorians* sought to puncture the reputations of such respected Brits as Florence Nightingale and General Gordon. Strachey faulted Nightingale for a variety of things, for he could not bear the 'gentle vision of female virtue which first took shape before the adoring eyes of the sick soldiers' in the Crimea, the sort of thing that led one to observe, 'Before she came, there was cussin' and swearin', but after that it was as 'oly as a church; the men kissed her shadow as it passed.' Instead, Strachey went out of his way to denigrate her for acting in an imperious manner when there was competition for primacy in the hospital; for the contempt she expressed for her medical colleagues in personal letters; for being slow to pick up on the work of Pasteur and Lister, laughing at their 'germ fetish'; and for her crafting an argument for God's existence (Laws of

---

4   Christopher Hitchens, Richard Dawkins, Sam Harris and Daniel Dennett, *The Four Horsemen: The Conversation That Sparked An Atheist Revolution* (New York: Random House, 2019), 125-126.

nature must have a lawgiver), which John Stuart Mill found lacking.[5]

In this, he echoed the spirit of another despiser of the 'pious' Victorian age, Samuel Butler. In *The Way of All Flesh*, Butler took delight in crafting the account of a minister who felt obliged to thrash his young son repeatedly for stumbling on pronunciation. The child was 'very late in being able to sound a hard "c" or "k," and, instead of saying, "Come," he said, "Tum, tum, tum."' Treating his mispronunciation as a willful act,

> he lugged the little wretch, crying by anticipation, out of the room. A few minutes more and we could hear screams coming from the dining-room, cross the hall which separated the drawing-room from the dining-room, and knew that poor Ernest was being beaten. 'I have sent him to bed,' said Theobald, as he returned to the drawing-room, 'and now, Christiana, I think we will have the servants to prayers,' and he rang the bell for them, red-handed as he was.[6]

At the very least, we need to take many of these accounts with a large grain of salt, whether they be Benedict-positive or Nightingale-negative.

---

5   Lytton Strachey, *Eminent Victorians* (New York: Penguin Modern Library, 1933), 151-190.

6   Samuel Butler, *The Way of All Flesh*, edited by James Cochrane (Harmondsworth, Middlesex, England: Penguin, 1903, Reprinted 1971), 124-125.

We should note that Christians, and not just atheists, can be adept at piling on examples for sectarian purposes. As terrible as it was, the Spanish Inquisition has been appropriated, magnified, and distorted by and for many causes. For one thing, in that era, the Protestant nations of Europe were determined to put Catholic Spain in the worst light. England would soon face the Spanish Armada, and the Netherlands would strive in the Eighty Years' War to cast off Spanish rule. If the enemy could be cast as savage tyrants, then the need for resistance was all the more compelling. Furthermore, Catholics in Italy were interested in freeing themselves from the domination of Catholics from Spain, so they joined in the defamation. Subsequently, Spanish secularists blamed the Inquisition for the economic and cultural retardation of their nation. And even the most earnest chroniclers could be twisted about by the lore that had found its way into source materials. Thus, generation after generation joined in the piling on, including the artist Goya and the Russian novelist Tolstoy.[7] And it may surprise some that the total number of executions ran to only around 3,000,[8] the same as died in the course of an hour in the Twin Towers on September 11, 2001.

---

7   Henry Kamen, *The Spanish Inquisition: A Historical Revision*, Fourth Edition (New Haven: Yale, 2014), chapter 15, 'Inventing the Inquisition.'

8   Kamen, 253.

SCHOLARS

Early Christians were sometimes accused of cannibalism, because they were 'eating the body of Christ' and of incest, because a man went home to be with his wife, his *sister* in Christ. In the 1890s, Andrew Dickson White, historian and president of Cornell University, repeatedly slandered the faith in his *A History of the Warfare of Science and Theology in Christendom*, saying, for example, that pastors once opposed the use of anesthesia in childbirth because it would mitigate the pain of the Genesis 3 curse.

The contributors to *Galileo Goes to Jail and Other Myths About Science and Religion* take White to task for this and other offenses. Scorched by being deemed an infidel, he retaliated with the conviction that 'In all modern history, interference with Science in the supposed interest of religion—no matter how conscientious such interference may have been—has resulted in the direst evils both to Religion and Science, and *invariably.*' He found a ready audience, including suffragist Elizabeth Cady Stanton, who counted his work evidence 'that the Bible has been the greatest block in the way of progress.'[9]

Despite Stanton's exultation, White is duly faulted for his conceits, which rest on the thinnest of sources. For instance, though he claimed that medieval Christians opposed

---

9   *Galileo Goes to Jail, and Other Myths About Science and Religion*, edited by Ronald L. Numbers (Cambridge: Harvard, 2009), 1-2.

dissection because it desecrated the 'temple of the soul,' the facts shouted otherwise:

> Most medieval church authorities not only tolerated but encouraged the opening and dismemberment of human corpses to religious ends: the embalming of holy bodies by evisceration; their division to yield corporeal relics; the inspection of the internal organs of holy men and women for signs of sanctity; and the operation that came later to be known as caesarean section, whose aim was to baptize fetuses extracted from the bodies of women who died in childbirth.[10]

Yes, there were limits and scruples, 'But these limits reflected secular values of personal and family honor and ritual decorum and were enforced by local governments rather than by religious authorities.'

In other chapters, White is faulted for falsely suggesting that Giordano Bruno, the sixteenth-century apostate priest, was executed for his heliocentric view of the universe, rather than his advocacy for an occult version of deism and universalism.[11] (The real story is bad enough, but White's misuse of it to serve his narrative makes it worse.)

To be fair, the 'myths' can serve the Christian camp as well. While giving some credit to Alfred North Whitehead's

---

10 Katharine Park, 'That the Medieval Church Prohibited Human Dissection,' in *Galileo Goes to Jail*, 44-45.

11 Jole Shackelford, 'That Giordano Bruno Was the First Martyr of Modern Science,' in *Galileo Goes to Jail*, 60-62.

claim that modern science grew out of medieval theology, Noah Efron insists that other cultures made substantial contributions.

> Modern science rests (somewhat, anyway) on early-modern, Renaissance, and medieval philosophies of nature, and these rested (somewhat, anyway) on Arabic natural philosophy, which rested (somewhat, anyway) on Greek, Egyptian, Indian, Persian, and Chinese texts, and these rested, in turn, on the wisdom generated by other, still earlier cultures.[12]

This is a model of academic hedging, but the point is that one must be wary of sweeping narratives, whoever is casting them. And, for purposes of this book, particular focus should fall on stories crafted to demean Christianity.

LANGUAGE GAMES

While narratives can be fashioned to cast people in an unwarranted favorable or unfavorable light, public relations experts and clever critics have a more fundamental tool at their disposal: word crafting, whether in the form of euphemism, or its opposite, dysphemism (substituting a word with harsh connotations for a more neutral expression). Logicians warn against 'question-begging epithets,' the use of loaded words to win your case without having to really make a good argument; it involves the employment of emotionally-

---

12 Noah J. Efron, 'That Christianity Gave Birth to Modern Science,' in *Galileo Goes to Jail*, 85.

charged talk to rig the outcome of an argument, whether by enchantment or bullying. (By the way, the popular use of the expression, 'begs the question,' is meant as a substitute for 'raises the question,' but that's not the formal meaning.)

Consider, for instance, the difference between asking, 'Do you think it's good to have a staff *populated* by so many evangelicals?' and 'Do you think it's a good thing to have a staff *infested* by so many evangelicals?' The former is an open question, while the second is not, for who can affirm an infestation? In other words, once you buy the vocabulary, you buy the perspective.

The Bible speaks to this in Isaiah 5:20: 'Woe to those who call evil good and good evil, who put darkness for light and light for darkness, who put bitter for sweet and sweet for bitter.' It's apt counsel for our day as well, when those who dare to quote the Bible in public policy discussions are called 'theocrats,' when Christians who repeat tough counsel from Scripture can be dismissed as 'Bible thumpers' or 'hellfire and brimstone' enthusiasts, and when sins are euphemized, with adultery called an 'affair.' We need to be wary of granting the critic's charge that we do 'bad' things when they have so poor a grasp of what's bad and good to begin with.

I'm reminded of a dust-up a number of years ago when New York Knicks, Charley Ward and Allan Houston, tried to win to Christ a Jewish reporter who was sitting in on a

Bible study with them. A Chicago columnist went ballistic when she read this, condemning the players for '[babbling] words of hate and nonsense' and calling Ward 'an insidious brand of bigot.' She, like many others, tossed around the words 'hate' and 'bigot' quite freely, and Christians often bear the brunt of this attack when they're merely presenting the biblical alternative to whatever the culture is pushing or indulging.

One of the most popular rhetorical ploys to batter Christianity is to appropriate a clinical expression, 'phobia' or 'phobe,' to cast devotees of traditional faith and practice as psychological defectives needing therapy and quarantine, rather than respect and a fair hearing. With it, one can turn a reasonable person into a pitiable object. On this model, the person who objects to the conceits of gender fluidity (a 'transphobe') is as irrational as an acrophobe (terrified by heights) or an agoraphobe (anxious in public places). Never mind that thoughtful people can suggest that a girls' track meet should exclude a sprinter with male chromosomes and genitalia, even though he self-identifies as female. If this stigma is allowed to stand, then a morally-sensible objection could be counted as one more 'bad thing' to be added to the list of bad things Christians do.

CULTURAL RELATIVISTS

In some regions, cultural relativists have been scandalized by the 'invasion' of upsetting Christian perspectives into the animistic world, and the government has gotten involved in protecting indigenous people from the preachments of missionaries. By their lights, tribal religion is the glue that holds these people together. Never mind that the fate of their eternal souls is in the balance, a fact that secularists hold in contempt. Never mind that their traditional practices involve serious transgressions and dangers; instead, relativists romanticize these people and leave them vulnerable to gospel-ignorance.

Of course, missionaries have done unfortunate things. So have philosophers, doctors and dietitians. But their core effort, to introduce people to Jesus Christ, 'The Way, the Truth, and the Life,' is admirable. Yet cultural relativists call it 'bad.'

CARICATURES

One way the critic gains purchase against Christianity is by playing the card of caricature, relying upon easy assumptions ingrained by years of unfair usage. Occasionally, Christian scholars will push back, setting the record straight. For instance, in *Worldly Saints: The Puritans As They Really*

Were,[13] Leland Ryken plays off the conventional wisdom in propositions beginning with 'Everybody Knows That the Puritans Were …' In turn, he addresses the supposition that they: 1. 'were against sex'; 2. 'never laughed and were opposed to fun'; 3. 'wore drab, unfashionable clothes'; 4. 'were opposed to sports and recreation'; 5. 'were money-grubbing workaholics who would do anything to get rich'; 6. 'were hostile to the arts'; 7. 'were overly emotional and denigrated reason'; 8. were likely 'over seventy suffering from tired blood'; 9. 'were repelled by the human body and the physical world'; 10. 'were intolerant toward people who disagreed with them'; 11. were 'overly strict'; 12. were a people who 'repressed normal human feelings in the name of religion'; 13. 'were legalistic moralists who judged people by their external behavior only'; 14. were the sort who 'indulged in much self-loathing'; 15. 'were ignorant people who opposed education.'

Quite a bill of indictment, but Ryken puts things in perspective. For one thing, he explains that the black garb was for Sundays and special occasions and that 'daily dress was colorful.' For instance, 'The American Puritan William Brewster wore a blue coat, a violet coat, and a green waistcoat.' Furthermore, John Owen of Oxford had a 'velvet jacket, breeches set round at knees with ribbons … and

---

13 Leland Ryken, *Worldly Saints: The Puritans As They Really Were* (Grand Rapids: Zondervan/Academie, 1986).

Spanish leather boots with cambric tops.' And regarding tolerance, the Puritan Oliver Cromwell, 'permitted the Jews to return to England and to have their own synagogue and cemetery in London.'

ATHEISTS' TESTIMONY FOR THE DEFENSE

An interesting source for counter narratives lies outside the Christian fold. Penn Jillette, an avowed atheist, is the tall one who talks in the magic and comedy duo, Penn and Teller.

A few years ago, Jillette recorded a short video about an audience member who came to talk to him after one of his shows. The man complimented Jillette on the performance and then said, 'I brought this for you' as he held up a small New Testament with the Psalms, one in which he had written a bit in the front. Jillette, moved by the man's gesture, recalled:

> He was kind, and nice, and sane, and looked me in the eyes, and talked to me, and then gave me this Bible. I've always said I don't respect people who don't proselytize. I don't respect that at all. If you believe there is a heaven and hell, and people could be going to hell or not getting eternal life or whatever, and you think it's not really worth telling them this because it would make it socially awkward. How much do you have to hate somebody to not proselytize? How much do you have to hate someone to believe everlasting life is possible and not tell them that?

Jillette then offered this analogy: 'If I believed, beyond a shadow of a doubt, that a truck was coming at you, and you didn't believe it, that that truck was bearing down on you, there's a certain point that I tackle you, and this is more important than that.' And he observed, 'This guy was a really good guy. He was polite, honest, and sane, and he cared enough about me to proselytize and give me a Bible.'

Now, Jillette is still an atheist, and he wanted to make that clear:

> I know there's no God, and one polite person living his life right doesn't change that. But I'll tell you, he was a very, very, very good man. And that's really important. And with that kind of goodness, it's okay to have that deep of a disagreement. I still think religion does a lot of bad stuff, but, man, that was a good man who gave me that book. That's all I wanted to say.[14]

A range of other atheists have spoken warmly of the influence of Christianity on cultures. Writing in *The Times*, Matthew Parris said, 'Removing Christian evangelism from the African equation may leave the continent at the mercy of a malign fusion of Nike, the witch doctor, the mobile phone and the machete.'[15] Though he would have preferred a more secular answer, he'd come to the conclusion, 'Education and

---

14 Penn Jillette, 'A Gift of a Bible,' YouTube video. https://www.youtube.com/watch?v=6md638smQd8

15 Matthew Parris, 'As an Atheist, I Truly Believe Africa Needs God,' *The Times* online, December 27, 2008: https://www.thetimes.

training alone will not do it. In Africa Christianity changes people's hearts. It brings a spiritual transformation. The rebirth is real. The change is good.'

And then there's Ayaan Hirsi Ali, who fled Muslim oppression in Somalia, rose to membership in the Dutch Parliament, helped make a film about the mistreatment of women in Islam, and was once again forced to flee Muslim oppression, this time from Europe. Identifying as an atheist, she observed, 'Given the choice, I would far rather live in a Christian than a Muslim country. Christianity in the West today is more humane, more restrained, and more accepting of criticism and debate.'[16]

Also, a word from American columnist and television commentator, S. E. Cupp, commending a believer's work:

> I am an atheist. I have been an atheist for fifteen years. And so my approach to this book insofar as it is a defense of Christianity is not one from within the structure but from outside it. I'm not propping up a particular faith because it is my own, but because I believe in those five important tenets—that Judeo-Christian values, religious tolerance, an objective

co.uk/article/as-an-atheist-i-truly-believe-africa-needs-god-3xj9bm80h8m (accessed December 29, 2018).

16 Ayaan Hirsi Ali, *Nomad: From Islam to America: A Personal Journey Through the Clash of Civilizations* (New York: Free, 2010), 240.

press, the benevolence of Christianity, and civility and decency make for a better democracy.[17]

SUMMARY OF MAIN POINTS

- The entertainment industry, the press, the literary world, and academia often misrepresent Christians, more typically putting them in a negative light. Believers and unbelievers alike can be duped.

- Just as narratives can skew perceptions, so too can the choice of vocabulary. Let the linguistic buyer beware.

- Cultural relativists are dismayed by the exclusive truth claims of Christianity, and they work to limit the spread of such troublesome 'nonsense.'

- It may come as a surprise, but non-believers can step forward to sing the praises of Christians, swimming upstream against the defamation that so often afflicts the Church.

---

17 S.E. Cupp, *Losing Our Religion: The Liberal Media's Attack on Christianity* (New York: Threshold, 2010), 10.

8

Who's Counting?

One of the most odious forms of argument is the glib pronouncement of 'moral equivalence,' both lame and pernicious, based on anecdote, oblivious to the vast differences that exist between and among rivals. It often comes in the form of *tu quoque* ('you, too') argument, a classic fallacy of reasoning. The problem here is twofold:

1. The fact that your opponent did something bad doesn't excuse you from doing something bad, so don't change the subject;

2. The 'too' is often absurd, in that there's no comparison between the two offenses, either in gravity or frequency, or both. The arguer presumes to play a trump card, which is nothing but a counterfeit held up the sleeve.

FAIR COMPARISONS

Yes, comparisons have their place. Writing in *The Illustrated London News*, December 14, 1907, G.K. Chesterton observed:

> When people impute special vices to the Christian Church, they seem entirely to forget that the world (which is the only other thing there is) has these vices much more. The Church has been cruel; but the world has been much more cruel. The Church has plotted; but the world has plotted much more. The Church has been superstitious; but it has never been so superstitious as the world is when left to itself.

Surprisingly, Sam Harris, a virulent atheist, has no patience for the sort of leveling so popular in the enlightened culture. In discussing whether all religions are equally bad, he observed, in response to Richard Dawkins' query 'whether Islam is worse than Christianity':

> It seems to me that we fail to enlist the friends we have on this subject when we balance this. It's a media tactic, and it's almost an ontological commitment of atheism, to say that all faith claims are in some sense equivalent. The media says the Muslims have their extremists and we have our extremists. There are jihadists in the Middle East and we have people killing abortion doctors. And that's just not an honest equation. The mayhem that's going on under the aegis of Islam just cannot be compared to the fact that we have two people a decade who kill abortionists. And this is one of the problems I have with the practice of atheism: it

hobbles us when we have to seem to spread the light of criticism equally in all directions at all moments, whereas we could, on some questions, have a majority of religious people agree with us.

A majority of people in the United States clearly agree that the doctrine of martyrdom in Islam is appalling and not at all benign, and liable to get a lot of people killed, and that is worthy of criticism. Likewise the doctrine that souls live in Petri dishes: even most Christians, 70 per cent of Americans, don't want to believe that, in light of the promise of embryonic stem-cell research. So it seems to me that once we focus on particulars, we have a real strength in numbers, and yet when we stand on the ramparts of atheism and say it's all bogus, we've lost 90 per cent of our neighbors.[1]

In that vein, let me construct an example to underscore the point. Say we produce a documentary on ISIS atrocities: setting a prisoner on fire; throwing homosexuals to their death from a tower; beheading Christians on the seashore. In response, a well-read ISIS representative comes back with, 'Have you ever heard of Dennis Rader?'

He's talking about a parishioner in good standing for years at Christ Lutheran Church in Wichita, Kansas. He'd even served as the president of the Church Council. But he

---

1   Christopher Hitchens, Richard Dawkins, Sam Harris and Daniel Dennett, *The Four Horsemen: The Conversation That Sparked An Atheist Revolution* (New York: Random House, 2019), 123.

became famous for murdering ten people over a seventeen year period and taunting the police with notes signed 'BTK' (for 'Bind, Torture, Kill'). Once caught, his penalty was 175 years in prison, with no possibility of parole. So, see, Christians do awful things too.

And what about George Metesky from Waterbury, Connecticut? In 1940, this 'Mad Bomber' was setting off explosions around New York; at the Consolidated Edison building, the New York Public Library, Grand Central Station and Radio City Music Hall. He also attended mass regularly. Consider, too, the Houston woman, Andrea Yates, who drowned her five children (aged six months to seven years) in a bathtub, for she was determined to save them from hell. She was convinced that Satan was influencing them and that they were developing improperly, so she needed to kill them before they would be accountable for sin, thus ensuring that they would go to heaven.

But surely there's a difference between an anomaly or rarity and a commonality or regularity? When asked to write a piece on the tenth anniversary of 9/11, I came across an account of attacks by Muslim terrorists over the past two months, and it occurred to me that every letter of the alphabet had at least one representative, giving me an interesting selection from among hundreds in the same time period: from Abuja (Nigeria) to Zarqa (Jordan), with even a Q (Quetta, Pakistan) and an X (Xingjian, China) along the way. So yes, both Lutherans and Muslims do bad things, but the incidence is vastly different. And while Lutherans, as a group, are ashamed of their fellow members' transgressions, ISIS proudly publicizes its atrocities.

Yes, many claim that the members of ISIS are only nominally Muslim, just as we would say that Rader and Metesky are not real Lutherans or Catholics, but this can be a tough case to make. After all, Mohammed, unlike Jesus: 1. himself bore the sword for the sake of advancing his faith's interests; 2. spawned a religion whose 'early church' (within a hundred years of his death), used military might to subjugate territory extending over two thousand miles west across North Africa and up into Europe, two thousand miles east to India, over five hundred miles south to Yemen, and over a thousand miles north into the Caucasus; 3. penned scripture (Quran 9:5) demanding violence toward and subjugation of their enemies:*'And when the forbidden months have passed, kill the idolaters wherever you find them and take them prisoners, and beleaguer them, and lie in wait for them at every place of ambush. But if they repent and observe Prayer and pay the Zakat, then leave their way free. Surely, Allah is Most Forgiving, Merciful.'*

Now, of course, the vast majority of Muslims don't belong to ISIS or one of the many other jihadist groups (for example, Boko Haram, the Taliban, Al-Qaeda, Al-Shabaab, Hizbul Mujahideen, Hezbollah, Abu-Sayyaf, al-Jama'a al-Islamiyya, Ansar Bangla, Darul Islam and Laskar Jundullah). But that's beside the point. Rader was a contemptible outlier within his own Wichita Church, as well as within his denomination, the Evangelical Lutheran Church in America, in a way that ISIS leader Abu Bakr al-Baghdadi was not despised within his own 'local church' (in Iraq and Syria) or his broader 'denomination' (extending to ISIS in Yemen), not to mention his extensive Muslim fan base beyond the ranks of ISIS.

But what about the non-sensational murders by Lutherans, or, for that matter, the non-sensational murders by non-terrorist Muslims? Shouldn't those be factored in? Well, whatever the journalistic practices might be in Muslim-majority countries, the Western press is disinclined to ignore the crimes of faithful churchgoers, as the contrast between Christian profession and awful behavior makes for enticing stories. Journalists favor a 'man bites dog' report over a 'dog bites man' story, so it is not reasonable to suppose that newspapers are nonchalant when it comes to publishing a piece on a homicidal deacon or a shoplifting nun.

University of Connecticut Sociologist, Bradley Wright, underscored the point of rarity in his book, *Christians Are Hate-Filled Hypocrites ... and Other Lies You've Been Told*:

> Essentially, people who associate themselves with Christianity, as compared to the religiously unaffiliated, are more likely to have faithful marriages, commit less

crime, interact honestly with others, and not get into as much trouble with drugs or alcohol. What's more, the more committed Christians are to their faith, as measured by church attendance, the greater the impact the church's teachings seem to have on their lives.[2]

To be fair, sometimes Muslims outshine Christians in certain regions. As Christopher Hitchens observed:

> I saw, myself, during the wars post-Yugoslavia, the Bosnian Muslims behaving far better than the Christians, either Catholic or Orthodox. They were the victims of religious massacres and not the perpetrators of them, and they were the ones who believed the most in multiculturalism. So it can happen. You could even meet people who said they were atheist Muslims, or Muslim atheists.[3]

But, as Hitchens notes, when he says, 'It can happen,' this is not the norm.

So, who's counting? The simple answer is that we all should be: numbers reflect important realities.

2   Bradley R. E. Wright, *Christians are Hate-Filled Hypocrites … and Other Lies You've Been Told: A Sociologist Shatters Myths from the Secular and Christian Media* (Minneapolis: Bethany House, 2010), 152.

3   Christopher Hitchens, Richard Dawkins, Sam Harris and Daniel Dennett, *The Four Horsemen: The Conversation That Sparked An Atheist Revolution* (New York: Random House, 2019), 101-102.

AND THEN THERE'S COMMUNISM

In the Harvard Press volume, *The Black Book of Communism: Crimes, Terror, Repression*,[4] the authors catalog the carnage visited on the world by Marxist-Leninist enthusiasts. The death toll includes the destruction of four million Ukrainians and two million others by means of artificial and systematically-perpetuated famine from 1932 to 1933; the Khmer Rouge's deportation and extermination of the urban population of Cambodia from 1975 to 1978, with a million executions and another million or so deaths from malnutrition or brutal prison conditions; the starvation of at least thirty million Chinese under Mao Tse-Tung; the death of 3 million North Koreans (out of a population of 23 million) from purges, concentration camp horrors and a war of aggression against South Korea; the execution of over fifteen thousand Cubans by the Castro regime along with the imprisonment of another 100,000 citizens; a death toll of 25,000 at the hands of Peru's Maoist 'Shining Path' terrorists.

As *New York Times'* reporter and 'Bolsheviki' apologist Walter Duranty put it in 1933, '[Y]ou can't make an omelette without breaking eggs.' Indeed. Stalin's omelet was brutally

---

4   Stephane Courtois, Nicolas Werth, Andrzej Paczkowski, Karel Bartosek, Jean-Louis Margolin, translated by Jonathan Murphy and Mark Kramer, consulting editor Mark Kramer, *The Black Book of Communism: Crimes, Terror, Repression* (Cambridge: Harvard University Press, 1999).

made: consider, for example, the June 1921 directives to help 'pacify' Russia's Tambov Province: 'District and Regional Political Commissions are hereby authorized to pronounce sentence on any village where arms are being hidden, and to arrest hostages and shoot them if the whereabouts of the arms are not revealed' and 'Wherever arms are found, execute immediately the eldest son in the family.'[5]

Again, as Chesterton put it, 'The Church has been cruel; but the world has been much more cruel.' So it's instructive to lay the above-mentioned Communist figures (over forty million from a fifty-year period) alongside the deaths resulting from 'Christian' ventures, over two millennia, from the Crusades (2 million over a 200-year period) to the European witch trials (perhaps fifty thousand spread over three centuries), and the contrast is striking.

COUNTING FRUIT

A decade ago, a hundred or so of us met at a retreat center in Europe to talk about the striking decline of the Church on the continent at a time when the Islamic presence was growing dramatically. Our *Kairos Journal* team (kairosjournal. org) contributed a booklet to the proceedings, *Legatees of a Great Inheritance*.[6] It reminded us all of the Judeo-

---

5   Ibid., 116.

6   Legatees of a Great Inheritance: How the Judeo-Christian Tradition Has Shaped the West (Kairos Journal, 2008). Accessible online at

Christian contributions to Western Civilization, including the establishment of hospitals and universities; the rise of modern science; the establishment of governmental checks and balances; the status of women and child labor laws; and the flourishing of the architecture.

About that same time, I read a list of recommended charities in *USA Today*, prompts to year-end giving for tax deduction purposes. As I did a little background reading, I discovered that most were founded by those professing faith in Christ: for example, the Red Cross, Habitat for Humanity, and Special Olympics. And I was reminded of the point raised in Vienna, that the Church has blessed and secured the best of our culture in countless ways; if you marginalize, demean, or persecute it, you will be astonished and saddened at what you lose.

So yes, let's count the cost of the various competing worldviews.

THE SCORING SCALE

Evaluative scales are fascinating. In judging Olympic divers, seven judges assign scores of 1 to 10, assessing such items as take-off from the platform and entry into the water. Then the top two best and worst scores are discarded and the remaining three are added together and multiplied by

https://www.kairosjournal.org/misc/FINAL.%20Legatees%20of%20a%20Great%20Inheritance.pdf.

the dive's difficulty rating. The Richter scale for judging the power of earthquakes works exponentially, with each higher number representing gain by a factor of 10 (with those scoring 4.5 capable of detection all around the world), and the Saffir-Simpson hurricane wind-speed scale runs from a Category 1 (74-95 mph) to Category 5 (over 157 mph). Notice that, given human capabilities and the laws of nature, diving judges don't insist on a fifty-foot bounce off the board and ten spins in the air before granting a 10; seismologists don't assign a Richter rating of 4.5 to the minor ground shake within a quarter mile of an eight-story building's implosion; Category 5 hurricanes don't start at 500 mph. To do so would be arbitrary and nonsensical.

Similarly, we need to use the proper scale in judging what forms of religion and irreligion are good or bad. Of course, with so many variables and value judgments involved, there is no precise Richter scale for such calls, but there is a wealth of statistical and anecdotal information which, taken together, arguably favors cultures with strong Christian influence, whether that influence is current or historic. I'll mention one indicator: the flow of immigration. Which nations have built walls and fences to keep their people in? On the other hand, which have labored to secure their borders against a massive influx of immigrants and have dealt with long waiting lists of those wishing entry? From where have people fled extreme poverty, oppression, lawlessness, corruption and/or endless warfare? Toward which lands have they voted with their feet? I submit that the magnet lands are historically saturated with Christian perspectives, notwithstanding their past and present sins.

PHILOSOPHER KINGS?

Even if immigration patterns suggest honor for societies shaped substantially by Christians (and, I would argue that Protestant shaping has been more beneficial than Roman Catholic shaping, as evidenced by the surge of refugees from Latin America north to the United States), might we still be setting our sights too low? What if the valid comparison is not with Communist and Muslim cultures, but rather with an ideal society not yet realized? After all, Christians claim to be wonderful 'salt and light' for the world, so why settle for less? Isn't there still room for embarrassment, even shame, when 'Christendom' is laid side by side with the ideal?

If so, what might that ideal be? Plato proffered an answer. In Book VI of *The Republic*, he prescribed rule by philosophers, those who exercised the clear thinking that took them beyond the hurly-burly madness of this world to the ideals which informed their enlightened choices. It sounds grand, but I think it would be a disaster to turn the keys of state over to the philosophers, putting the bureaucracy, the police and the army into their hands. (I write this on the eve of a gathering of the American Philosophical Association, where

I'm scheduled as a commentator for a paper in ethics. As I look through the program, I find a wild range of opinions in play, many of them toxic and even congenial to tyrannies in centuries past.) And I would say the same for 'Sociologist Kings,' 'Psychologist Kings,' 'Economist Kings,' 'Historian Kings,' 'Artist Kings,' and 'Literature Professor Kings'—or, for that matter, a round table of 'Academician Kings.' (I raise this concern since the title question of this book is far more typical of the academy than the barbershop, union hall, or military base.) This sort of reservation prompted William Buckley to declare, cheekily, 'I would rather be governed by the first 2,000 people in the Boston phone book than by the faculty of Harvard.'

And no, the answer is not to enthrone 'Clergy Kings,' for the Bible does not prescribe theocracy for our day. Indeed, it discourages it, calling upon us to render to Caesar that which is his. So let us lay aside the notion that Christians should pay homage to non-Christian utopias or join in the quest for some sort of neutral dreamland. For, again, we're working with people, and Christian people (whether academics or not) are works in progress, not susceptible to perfection this side of heaven.

SUMMARY OF MAIN POINTS

*   When a body of believers is being evaluated in an imperfect world, it's fair to make comparisons. There's

a difference between lonely cases and overwhelming numbers.

- For instance, the track record of Christianity compares quite favorably with that of Islam and Communism.
- Counting should focus on more than negatives; it's also important to count the positives.
- It's fair to ask what alternative ideal or utopia the critic might have in mind when disparaging Christianity— and then to scrutinize that alternative for plausibility.

9

Antibodies: Devotional and Congregational

Any time you have humans at work and play in the world, you'll find evil deeds, Christian activities not excepted. But there is a major difference in how things are set straight. The Allies overthrew the Third Reich, and the Hindu practice of widow-burning was banned in India, with the advocacy of Christian missionary, William Carey. (Of course, subsequent British rule was instrumental in the change. As British commanding general Sir Charles James Napier is reported to have said, 'This burning of widows is your custom; prepare the funeral pile. But my nation has also a custom. When men burn women alive we hang them, and confiscate all their property. My carpenters shall therefore erect gibbets on which to hang all concerned when the widow is consumed. Let us all act according to national customs.'[1])

As a rule, non-Christian tyrannies must be changed from the outside. They lack the immune systems to deal with their own moral diseases. As the AIDS epidemic well demonstrates, when one's internal defenses falter, the body can fall prey to all sorts of 'opportunistic infections,' including shingles, Karposi's sarcoma, salmonella, pneumonia and tuberculosis. It calls to mind the old saw, 'If you don't stand for something, you'll fall for anything.' And, of course, AIDS is just one version of this malady, a grouping that includes leukemia, multiple myeloma and viral hepatitis. They all leave the body vulnerable to ruin, and it takes something from outside (the 'other' of '*allo*pathic' medicine) to arrest the sickness, whether through antiretroviral chemotherapy, radiation, or surgery.

But Christians have a wealth of antibodies designed to fight infection: for example, the indwelling of the Holy Spirit, the written Word of God and the counsel of fellow believers. We see the British William Wilberforce and American Jonathan Blanchard (founder of Wheaton College) working hard, and with effect, to end the scourge of slavery in their respective nations. In the 1970s, we watch

---

1   William Francis Patrick Napier, *The History of General Sir Charles Napier's Administration of Scinde, and Campaign in the Cutchee Hills* (London: C. Westerton, 1851), 35.

Billy Graham lead in establishing the Evangelical Council for Financial Accountability to counteract the unscrupulous handling of funds within the Church.

One feature of a body with a healthy immune system is its responsiveness to vaccines, which introduce a trace of the disease to arouse antibodies for future fights. Thus we arm ourselves against a variety of diseases, drawing on the resources we already have in place: smallpox, polio, typhoid, rabies and measles, to name a few. I submit, analogously, that Christianity has flirted with some toxic stuff through the years, but these misadventures have served to clarify and strengthen the faith's opposition to such harmful foolishness.

Let's consider several of those means by which 'bad Christians' have received their cure.

DEVOTIONAL MATERIAL

First, much of the work of cleansing is done in the 'prayer closet.' Church history has provided the faithful a limitless supply of devotional material, designed to lead each soul into self-examination, pointing the way to edification. Here's one probing example from C. S. Lewis's *Mere Christianity*, which is also an apologetic book. You might call it the 'hatred test':

> For a long time I used to think this a silly, straw-splitting distinction: how could you hate what a man did and not hate the man? But years later it occurred to me that there was one man to whom I had been doing this all my life—namely myself. However much

I might dislike my own cowardice or conceit or greed, I went on loving myself ... Just because I loved myself, I was sorry to find that I was the sort of man who did those things.

Consequently, Christianity does not want to reduce by one atom the hatred we feel for cruelty and treachery. We ought to hate them. Not one word of what we have said about them needs to be unsaid. But it does want us to hate them in the same way in which we hate things in ourselves: being sorry that the man would have done such things, and hoping, if it is anyway possible, that somehow, sometime, somewhere, he can be cured and made human again.

The real test is this. Suppose one reads a story of filthy atrocities in the paper. Then suppose that something turns up suggesting that the story might not be quite true, or not quite so bad as it was made out. Is one's first feeling, 'Thank God, even they aren't quite so bad as that,' or is it a feeling of disappointment, and even a determination to cling to the first story for the sheer pleasure of thinking your enemies as bad as possible? If it is the second then it is, I am afraid, the first step in a process which, if followed to the end, will make us into devils. You see, one is beginning to wish that black was a little blacker.

If we give that wish its head, later on we shall wish to see grey as black and then to see white itself as black. Finally, we shall insist on seeing everything—God and our friends and ourselves included—as bad, and not be able to stop doing it: we shall be fixed for ever in a universe of pure hatred.[2]

PERSONAL REPENTANCE

In John 16:8, Jesus is recorded to have said that the Holy Spirit would 'prove the world to be in the wrong about sin and righteousness and judgment' … and that is what happened to Samuel Sewall, who was one of eight judges at the Salem witch trials that sent twenty to their death in 1692.[3] Five years later, he walked up the aisle of Boston's Third Church and stood as Pastor Willard read his confession: 'He desires to take the blame and shame of it … desiring prayers that God … would pardon that sin.'

Through the intervening years, he had been burdened by guilt, prayerful before God and especially stung by Matthew 12:7, which his son had recited in 1696: 'If ye had known what this meaneth, I will have mercy and not sacrifice, ye would not have condemned the guiltless.' For the rest of his life, he wore a hair shirt under his garments, and he wrote pieces against slavery and the mistreatment of women and Indians.

---

2   C.S. Lewis, *Mere Christianity* (New York: Touchstone/Simon & Schuster, 1980 [originally MacMillan, 1943]), 105-106.

3   Eve LaPlante, *Salem Witch Judge: The Life and Repentance of Samuel Sewall* (New York: HarperOne, 2007), 200.

Of course, the classic expressions of repentance are found in the Psalms, and believers have turned to them repeatedly for soul-cleansing contrition. Psalm 51 is particularly wrenching, as it expresses the brokenness of King David after the prophet Nathan had stung him with the accusation that he had arranged the destruction of Uriah, a general whose wife, Bathsheba, David had taken in adultery. Here's a selection from that Psalm, words that countless Christians have prayed, aware of their own wretchedness for the sinful particulars of their lives:

> [1] Have mercy on me, O God,
>   according to your unfailing love …
>
> [3] For I know my transgressions,
>   and my sin is always before me…
> [8] Let me hear joy and gladness;
>   let the bones you have crushed rejoice.
> [9] Hide your face from my sins
>   and blot out all my iniquity.
>
> [10] Create in me a pure heart, O God,
>   and renew a steadfast spirit within me.
> [11] Do not cast me from your presence
>   or take your Holy Spirit from me.
> [12] Restore to me the joy of your salvation
>   and grant me a willing spirit, to sustain me.
>
> [13] Then I will teach transgressors your ways,
>   so that sinners will turn back to you.
> [14] Deliver me from the guilt of bloodshed, O God,

you who are God my Savior,
     and my tongue will sing of your righteousness.
¹⁵ Open my lips, Lord,
     and my mouth will declare your praise.
¹⁶ You do not delight in sacrifice, or I would bring it;
     you do not take pleasure in burnt offerings.
¹⁷ My sacrifice, O God, is a broken spirit;
     a broken and contrite heart
     you, God, will not despise.

Personal Disciplines

A number of men, including Richard Foster, Dallas Willard and Donald Whitney, have written books on cultivating spiritual disciplines. In Whitney's book, he commends, for instance, fasting (voluntary abstinence from food for spiritual purposes) and silence and solitude (voluntarily and temporary withdrawal into privacy for spiritual purposes). Comparing the two, he observes,

> On a long fast you discover that much of the food you normally eat is really unnecessary. When you practice silence and solitude, you find that you don't need to say many things you think you need to say. In silence, we learn to rely more on God's control in situations where we would normally feel compelled to speak, or to speak too much. We find out that He is able to manage situations in which we once thought our input was indispensable. The skills of observation and listening are also sharpened in those who practice

silence and solitude so that when they do speak there's
more of a freshness and depth to their words.[4]

Throughout the book, he draws on the teaching of Scripture
(e.g. the period of Jesus' temptation in the wilderness, as He
gave Himself over to fasting and solitude); historical figures,
such as David Brainerd and a Scottish Olympic runner
named Allan Wells; and characters from literature, such as
the young lawyer in Anton Chekhov's short story, 'The Bet.'
All are woven together to encourage our use of 'God-given
means … in the Spirit-filled pursuit of Godliness.'

Scripture memorization is one of those disciplines. It
helps guard us against going off the spiritual and moral rails,
and thus helps us avoid societal contempt as well. But it can
also keep us from chasing after cultural foolishness, from
adopting fashions of thought and feeling that will not age
well.

In that connection, I'll mention an encounter I had
not long ago. I was attending a philosophy colloquium
at a private, secular university. The topic that day was
on 'intellectual humility' and dealing with 'testimonial
injustice.' The speaker played off a quote from the movie,
The Talented Mr. Ripley, one in which a wealthy man's

---

4   Donald Whitney, *Spiritual Disciplines for the Christian Life*
    (Colorado Springs: NavPress, 1991), 192. Whitney's list extends,
    as well, to Bible intake, prayer, worship, evangelism, serving,
    stewardship, journaling and learning.

girlfriend expressed suspicion over Ripley in the wake of his son's disappearance, to which he responded, 'Marge, there's female intuition and then there are facts.'

The speaker then sketched out an account of how the lady had been harmed by his dismissive, sexist remark. Indeed, as the paper declared, she had been the victim of injustice, one more instance of an overarching structural problem, whereby people are encouraged to short-change themselves and others because of their race, class and sexual orientation.

Okay, there's value here, but I didn't feel good about her readiness to 'go nuclear' in her assessment of verbal slights. I saw this as one more brick in the wall of cultivated indignation, the disposition to be ever alert to 'micro-aggressions' as a 'social justice warrior.' (It reminded me a bit of the obsession with 'honor' I'd observed in the Middle East, where jails were filling up with young women in protective custody, girls made safe from relatives who'd been 'disgraced' by their neglect of or defiance toward the family's religious sensitivities.) So there in the colloquium, I raised my hand and brought up my own situation as one turning seventy.

I asked the speaker to imagine that I'd advised some millennials to think of taking an umbrella to a ball game, only to have them roll their eyes, offer up patronizing smiles, and assure me, 'Thanks. We've got this' (meaning that they were ignoring the advice of an overly-cautious old coot). I suggested that if this should happen, I was neither harmed nor treated unjustly. It was their problem, not mine, if they got soaking wet. I didn't need everybody to take my word as law or to think I was some sort of sage.

And then Scripture passages came to mind. I'll mention a half-dozen off the top of my head. Because I'd intentionally or incidentally learned them through the decades, they were handy to frame my take on the paper:

1. Instead of the maxim, 'Don't get mad. Get even,' turn instead to Matthew 5:38-40: 'You have heard that it was said, "Eye for eye, and tooth for tooth," But I tell you, do not resist an evil person. If anyone slaps you on the right cheek, turn to them the other cheek also. And if anyone wants to sue you and take your shirt, hand over your coat as well.'

2. You should be willing to 'Bless those who curse you, pray for those who mistreat you' (Luke 6:28).

3. Instead of obsessing over the esteem in which we're held (or lack thereof), we might recall 1 Corinthians 1:26-27:

   > Brothers and sisters, think of what you were when you were called. Not many of you were wise by human standards; not many were influential; not many were of noble birth. But God chose the foolish things of the world to shame the wise; God chose the weak things of the world to shame the strong.

Indeed, 'When we are slandered, we answer kindly. Up to this moment we have become the scum of the earth, the garbage of the world' (1 Cor. 4:13).

4. Consider the example of Jesus: 'In your relationship with one another, have the same mindset as Christ Jesus: Who being in very nature God, did not consider equality with God something to be used to his own advantage; rather, he made himself nothing by taking the very nature of a servant ….' (Phil. 2:5-7a).

5. And a little self-criticism can help: 'Why do you look at the speck of sawdust in your brother's eye and pay no attention to the plank in your own eye' (Matt. 7:3).

ACCOUNTABILITY GROUPS

While serving a seminary in the Midwest, I was invited to join with a local pastor, a hospital administrator and the director of a parachurch ministry in an accountability group, one that met for breakfast once a week. The fellowship was a real encouragement, but a holy awkwardness could set in as we got down to business around the small, ten-question cards we carried in our billfolds. One item at a time, we'd take turns responding to probing inquiries about our past week's financial dealings (including expense reports), stewardship of our eyes and descent into irritability. And just in case you fudged in your answers, the last question asked whether you'd lied on any of the others. (Of course, if you'd lied on

1-9, you were probably low enough to go ahead and lie on 10, but it was a good convictional prompt just the same.)

Of course, the supreme questioner, the Lord, didn't just meet us for breakfast once a week, but was ever present, but I'm convinced He used this little group to keep us fresh in our prayer lives. We all stumbled at some point or another and were manifestly imperfect, even deplorable at times, but the point was not whether this weekly exercise led us to full sanctification, but what we might have been had we not engaged in this effort to keep ourselves honest and clean.

SUNDAY WORSHIP GATHERINGS

When the 'whole counsel of God' is preached, conviction follows: 'For the word of God is living and active. Sharper than any double-edged sword, it penetrates even to dividing soul and spirit, joints and marrow; it judges the thoughts and attitudes of the heart' (Heb. 4:12).

Clovis Chappell, who was pastor of First Methodist Church of Charlotte, North Carolina, at his retirement in 1949, was notable for his stewardship of the pulpit. Here's an example of his work, where, in a **sermon**, he takes on the problem of unforgiveness, which can plague Christians, generating sins of both commission and omission. He works from Philippians 3:13-14: ' ... Forgetting what is behind and straining toward what is ahead, I press on toward the goal to win the prize for which God has called me heavenward in Christ Jesus.' With this base, he makes a number of applications, noting for one thing that we should not forget acts of kindness, occasions for gratitude. Still, there are some things we must throw away:

> Throw away the slights and insults that may come to you on the way. Collect old coins, if you like, or rare stamps, but don't collect grudges. I used to get a great many anonymous letters. Some of those letters were as sweet as honeysuckle. Some timid souls that felt that I had helped them were giving me a secret pat on the back. But most of them were the opposite. I think the bitterest one that I ever had was while I was pastor at First Church, Memphis. It was a terror. As I read it I could not but wonder how it got through the post office without setting it on fire. It should have been written on asbestos. Naturally as soon as I finished that poisonous letter I hurried to the bank to tuck it into my safe-deposit box. This I did so I could read it every morning to keep myself angry. 'Nobody,' you say, 'would be that foolish.' But millions are. They file away and keep that which will make them at once miserable and mean.'[5]

When one thinks of revival within the Church, images of 'the sawdust trail' surface, but God uses a wide range of instruments to renew His people. In August of 1742, 30,000 Scotsmen assembled in a natural outdoor amphitheater

---

5   Clovis Gillham Chappell, 'Great Living,' *20 Centuries of Great Preaching*, vol. 9 (Waco, Texas: Word, 1971), 233.

to hear the great preacher, George Whitefield. He'd come to the site at the invitation of locals who'd been gathering daily for months to pray and to hear the accounts of other works of God in what is called the First Great Awakening. Atypically, a **communion** service was held at the center of this meeting, with an estimated 10 per cent of the attendees, some 3,000, receiving the elements. Extra tents were set up to accommodate the observants.

Through **liturgy**, responsive reading and communal prayers, the gathered church says pointed and convicting things to reorder the soul. A classic in this genre is the confessional prayer found in the Anglican *Book of Prayer*:

> ALMIGHTY and most merciful Father; We have erred, and strayed from thy ways like lost sheep. We have followed too much the devices and desires of our own hearts. We have offended against thy holy laws. We have left undone those things which we ought to have done; And we have done those things which we ought not to have done; And there is no health in us. But thou, O Lord, have mercy upon us, miserable offenders. Spare thou those, O God, who confess their faults. Restore thou those who are penitent; According to thy promises declared unto mankind in Christ Jesus our Lord. And grant, O most merciful Father, for his sake; That we may hereafter live a godly, righteous, and sober life, To the glory of thy holy Name. Amen.

As they gather, Christians sing their words of thanks and praise, confession, aspiration, and resolve—through their **hymnody.** Among the classics is John Newton's 'Amazing Grace,' the testimony of a man once heavily involved in the British slave trade, but dramatically converted. Though few of us have been slavers (or murderers or burglars or adulterers), we track with his sentiments as we sing:

> Amazing grace! How sweet the sound
> That saved a wretch like me.
> I once was lost, but now am found,
> Was blind but now I see.

People disinclined to self-identify as 'wretches' have suggested alternative lyrics, replacing 'saved a wretch like me' with 'saved and set me free,' 'saved a soul like me,' or 'saved and strengthened me.' But those of us who know ourselves and will admit it sing the original words with conviction.

Of course, 'Amazing Grace' doesn't address moral specifics; rather it prompts and expresses brokenness over sin and guilt in general. But those who sing it sincerely can fill in the blanks in their minds (e.g., 'that saved a hateful/lustful/greedy/unforgiving/lazy/lying/gossiping/backstabbing/cowardly creep like me'). Thus, they enter into the shame and regret of the song, and rehearse their gratitude for Jesus' atonement on the cross and the regenerative power of the Holy Spirit in their lives.

Another hymn that expresses the Christian's sadness and repentance over sinful thought and behavior is 'Come Thou, Fount of Every Blessing':

> Prone to wander, Lord I feel it
> Prone to leave the God I love
> Here's my heart Lord, take and seal it
> Seal it for Thy courts above

For purposes of comparison, consider these words from *The International*, the first national anthem of the Soviet Union:

> No saviour from on high delivers
> No faith have we in prince or peer
> Our own right hand the chains must shiver
> Chains of hatred, greed and fear.

If such ungodly revolt goes off the rails morally, there will be no preacher urging forgiveness, no talk of wretches except about the ones who mistreated them ... so much for moral antibodies for this body.

COVENANTS

Churches often draw up covenants, principles of behavior by which the members bind themselves to one another. Some use Nehemiah 10 as inspiration. Back in Jerusalem following a period of Babylonian captivity, which they'd suffered for their waywardness, the Israelites heard a fresh reading of Scripture, renewed observance of the required

Festival of Booths, and they undertook a national confession of sins. Then, scores of leaders signed a binding agreement, which included Sabbath observance and Temple sacrifice.

Though Christians now observe the first day of the week, rather than the seventh, as their day of worship, and though there is no need for Temple sacrifice, now that Christ has made the once-for-all sacrifice, believers still focus on corporate worship and ceremonies in their covenants. For instance, members of the eighteenth-century Baptist Church in Caerleon, Wales, said they would 'endeavor to support and practice the ordinances of the gospel [the Lord's Supper and baptism] in their apostolic purity.' And in that same century, the Baptist Church in Kiokee, Georgia, promised 'as much as in our power to give all due attendance to the public worship of God on the Lord's Days.'

But the covenants also turned outward. Those in the Baptist Church in Horse Fair, Stony Stratford, Buckinghamshire, England, bound themselves to a pledge crafted in 1790, a covenant which included, 'To walk in a way and manner becoming of the gospel, before them that are without, that we may by well-doing put to silence the ignorance of gainsayers. We will practice the strictest honesty in our dealings, and faithfulness in fulfilling all our promises.[6]

---

6   These three representative covenants appear in *Baptist Confessions, Covenants, and Catechisms*, edited by Timothy and Denise George

CATECHISMS

Christian churches all across the denominational spectrum, from Catholic to Mennonite, employ catechisms, with perhaps the most famous being the two Westminster Catechisms. One particularly interesting one was written by Ann Judson, wife of Adoniram Judson, while the couple was serving as pioneer missionaries to Burma. She covers the doctrinal basics (e.g. 'Q. Where is God? A. God is everywhere, and living in His holy city in heaven.') and, like many others, includes treatment of the Ten Commandments in her version. She also lists obligations to observe such biblical counsel as 'Don't be slack. Be hardworking in whatever you do'; 'Do not take revenge on others when they abuse you; instead, love them with all your heart'; 'Be generous to the poor.'[7]

SOLEMN ASSEMBLIES

In the closing decades of the twentieth century, a range of churches and denominations took fresh notice of a biblical phenomenon, the solemn assembly. The prophet Joel calls for it in his second chapter, verses 15 to 17: 'Blow the trumpet in Zion, declare a holy fast, call a sacred assembly. Gather

---

(Nashville, B&H, 1996), pp. 171-224.

7   Tin Tin Aye and Jack McElroy, *Adoniram Judson's Soul Winning Secrets Revealed: An Inspiring Look at the Tools Used by 'Jesus Christ's Man' in Burma* (Shirley, Massachusetts: McElroy, 2013), [Kindle version] location 599-708.

the people ... Let the priests, who minister before the Lord weep ... Let them say, "Spare your people, O LORD."'

The prayer leaders of various Southern Baptist entities issued a call for such congregational gatherings, citing the leadership of Rehoboam, Asa, Jehoshaphat, Hezekiah, Josiah, Ezra and Nehemiah as well as Joel. They suggested an order of service for the assemblies, including particulars such as, 'Invite people to confess sin by standing if they have identified idols of the heart; then ask a leader to pray for cleansing, forgiveness, and restoration for those standing.' They also provided examples of the sorts of sins that might be robbing them of their spiritual health, including 'defaulting on a debt,' 'practicing prejudice or discrimination,' 'disgracing God's name in the eyes of the community,' 'failing to care for the needs of members, families, or couples,' and 'leaving the inner city for the suburbs rather than dealing with the problems of the people in the inner city.'

The point was that things had gotten so bad in the world, and within the Church, that desperate times called for desperate prayer and spiritual self-scrutiny. Jonathan Edwards sounded this note in an impressively entitled work, 'An Humble Attempt to Promote Explicit Agreement and Visible Union of God's People in Extraordinary Prayer, For the Revival of Religion and the Advancement of Christ's Kingdom on Earth.' And no, he wasn't calling for establishment of a caliphate or a global soviet or any such totalitarian regime, but rather the reign of the Holy Spirit in the lives of Jesus' followers. In calling for a concert of prayer, Edwards lamented, 'How much is the gospel-ministry grown into contempt!' and observed, 'Great discoveries have been made in the arts and sciences, and never was human learning carried to such a height, as in the present age; and yet never did the cause of religion and virtue run so low, in nations professing the true religion.'[8] Edwards' point was not to persecute the Church's gainsayers, but to join them sorrowfully in admitting the sorry state of affairs that had come upon it.

Having taken part in several of these exercises, I can testify that they can be excruciating and cleansing. In one case, as a seminary leader, I took my turn at the microphone to confess shortcomings that the Lord impressed on my mind, and, on another occasion, in preparation for a series of special meetings with a guest evangelist, I offered to visit and seek reconciliation with anyone in the congregation whom members brought to my attention. It's not a pleasant thing to visit the home of critics and opponents to seek forgiveness for needless offenses, leaving whatever reciprocal apologies there might be up to the Lord and the one to whom I was

---

8   Jonathan Edwards, 'An Humble Attempt &c.,' *The Works of Jonathan Edwards, Volume Two* (Edinburgh: Banner of Truth Trust, 1974 [first published 1834]), 293.

speaking. But it served to disarm us all in preparation for what proved to be an historic week of renewal in the church.

CHURCH DISCIPLINE

In his book, *Church Discipline: How the Church Protects the Name of Jesus*,[9] Jonathan Leeman notes that this practice (also called 'corrective' and 'formative') is grounded in the teachings of Jesus (Matt. 18:15-20) and Paul (1 Cor. 5:4-5). It's done for the sake of love, for the sake of the individual needing repentance and for the sake of observers, both within the church and among its neighbors, so that they might not be misled concerning the true nature of the faith and Christian life. The goal is not annihilation, but rather restoration. Neither is it an act of 'excommunication,' whereby the subject is supposedly cut off from salvation by virtue of separation from the church. And it's not done callously, presumptuously, or willy-nilly. Rather, it proceeds pastorally and quietly, moving to congregational action only when the sinners are *unrepentant* (when the sinner 'refuses to let go of the sin or fight against it'), *outward* ('can be seen and heard') and *significant* (leading the church 'to feel unable to continue affirming someone's profession of faith').

The gracious spirit of this action is also reflected in the seventeenth-century Anabaptist *Dordrecht Confession*

---

9   Jonathan Leeman, *Church Discipline: How the Church Protects the Name of* Jesus (Wheaton: Crossway, 2012).

(Article XVII), which speaks of the social 'shunning' of a member so expelled:

> [In] shunning as in reproving such offender, such moderation and Christian discretion be used, that such shunning and reproof may not be conducive to his ruin, but be serviceable to his amendment. For should he be in need, hungry, thirsty, naked, sick or visited by some other affliction, we are in duty bound, according to the doctrine and practice of Christ and His apostles, to render him aid and assistance, as necessity may require; otherwise the shunning of him might be rather conducive to his ruin than to his amendment (1 Thess. 5:14).

> Therefore we must not treat such offenders as enemies, but exhort them as brethren, in order thereby to bring them to a knowledge of their sins and to repentance; so that they may again become reconciled to God and the church, and be received and admitted into the same—thus exercising love towards them, as is becoming (2 Thess. 3:15).

This is, then, no Salman-Rushdie-like *fatwa*, but rather the dictate of love, albeit tough love.

Summary of Main Points

- Unlike groups which must be restrained from the outside, Christianity has internal mechanisms for correcting itself.

- Devotional writings, from the Psalms to the probing and inspiring work of Christian authors, provide the believer with a wealth of material to assess the condition of his or her own soul and take steps to improve his or her spiritual walk.

- The exercise of spiritual disciplines, such as fasting, journaling and scripture-memorizing, serves as both preventive medicine and surgery.

- From sermons, to hymns, to communion, to liturgical prayers, the classic elements of the church service can impact with mighty benefit the hearts of the congregants.

- Churches have a range of instruments and activities (including catechisms, covenants, solemn assemblies, accountability groups and disciplinary actions) to purify their witness and encourage healthy spiritual growth.

10

Antibodies: Beyond Home and Congregation

Christians also undertake self-corrective measures beyond the walls of home and the local church.

REVIVALS/AWAKENINGS

When spiritual renewal sweeps a nation or nations, it is often called an *awakening;* when it impacts primarily a local church or community, we generally use the term *revival,* whether it notes a transformative event or simply speaks hopefully of one, as when a congregation schedules a 'revival meeting.' But the terms have been used interchangeably.

These phenomena not only generate converts, but also elevate the manners and morals of society. Those familiar with world history may well have heard of the eighteenth-century Great Awakening in Britain and America (with Whitefield and Wesley as its leaders in England and

Jonathan Edwards in the colonies); the nineteenth-century's Second Great Awakening in the US (with Charles Finney in the North and the Sandy Creek Baptists in the South); the 1857–1858 Prayer Revival in New York; and the twentieth-century's Shantung Revival in China, which energized the life and work of missionaries, and brought myriad Chinese people to faith.

For our purposes, let's take a quick look at another twentieth-century work of God, this one beginning in Wales in 1904, when the preachers Evan Roberts and Seth Joshua led the nation to pray, 'Bend us, O Lord.' Thanks to the writing of J. Edwin Orr, many have come to learn of the 85,000 professions of faith and the many instances of social transformation which echoed around the world; for example, an absence of police bookings for drunkenness over the Christmas weekend in Swansea; a drop in illegitimate births in London; the pacification of a blood-thirsty tribe in Malawi; the return of stolen money and objects in Gujarat, India; repudiation of a range of sins in Kiating, China—'idolatry, theft, murder, adultery, gambling, opium smoking, disobedience to parents and hatred of employers, quarrelsomeness, lying, cheating, and the like were confessed for forgiveness.'[1]

---

1   J. Edwin Orr, *The Flaming Tongue: The Impact of Twentieth Century Revivals* (Chicago: Moody, 1973), 17, 49, 124, 152, 163.

Back in the late 1980s, as a pastor in Arkansas, I put together a collection of revival accounts from within the state, featuring one every twenty years or so, ranging back into the nineteenth century.[2] For instance, in 1864, at an encampment near Three Creeks, preaching and prayer meetings continued through the night around Confederate campfires, and as many as 500 made professions of faith in Christ. When an officer attempted to break up the gatherings with a 9:00 p.m. roll call, Chaplain Kavanaugh went to the Division Commander and asked if they might continue without this interruption. The General responded, 'Doctor, I will do anything in my power to promote this great reformation; for I assure you that since your meetings commenced I have not had a complaint entered against a single man in my army, and the people in the country have not been disturbed by a single soldier.'

Of course, it was good that the Rebel cause failed, that the nation was preserved and slavery abolished, but it is hard to gainsay the spiritual transformations that occurred in such Confederate camps and the blessings that stemmed from them in the post-war years. Chaplain Kavanaugh continued, 'After the army was disbanded, in riding through the country in Arkansas and Texas, I met with some of our

---

2   'Three Creeks—1864,' *Arkansas Baptist Revivals: A Sampler* (Little Rock: Evangelism Department, Arkansas Baptist State Convention: 1988).

converts, who had returned to their families and parents, and they were still true to their profession and evinced a decidedly firm Christian character. The parents of some of those young men have since told me that in place of having the characters and habits of their sons ruined by being in the army they had returned to them as happy Christian men.'[3] (Of course, God was working in the Union Camps as well, with, for instance, Dwight L. Moody's traveling far and wide to the units, ministering the gospel.)

Continuing on through the years, I came across stories about the dissolution of chronic enmity within congregations. For instance, in Mountain Pine, Arkansas, the breakups and subsequent remarriages of a certain couple had plagued the church with rancor ... that is, until they expressed sorrow and repentance for the spectacle they had visited upon the congregation. As one long-time member, Alta Lois Outler, put it, 'If a church is on fire for the Lord, problems bounce off in a hurry. If it's not on fire, any little problem is a mountain.'[4] By all accounts, this congregation's renewal was spurred by a 'Sunday School revival' in nearby Hot Springs, where some members were moved mightily.

---

3   Rev. J. Williams Jones, *Christ in the Camp or Religion in the Confederate Army* (Harrisburg, Virginia: Sprinkle Publications, 1887).

4   Quoted in collection of interviews under 'Mountain Pine—1987,' Mark Coppenger, *Arkansas Baptist Revivals: A Sampler*, 145.

Those unfamiliar with revivals might think that such sweet transformations were the result of feel-good messages, reminiscent of the famous Coca-Cola ad, where young people from around the world gathered, Cokes in hand, on a hillside in Italy, to join their voices: 'We'd like to teach the world to sing in perfect harmony …'

More typically, the preacher's message would be blunt. Indeed, Mordecai Ham, who was preaching when Billy Graham was saved, employed some sarcasm and parody to ridicule soft preaching. To do so, he appeared in winged collar, cutaway coat and kid gloves, carrying a little manuscript tied with a pink ribbon. Delivering what he called his 'pink sermon for tenderfoots,' he employed such expression as found in these excerpts:

> I would not shock the keen sensibilities of my noble auditors by so revolting and harrowing a story as the ugly crucifixion of one whose life was as mild as the gentle zephyr which plays with the refreshing mist rising from the picturesque little falls in the babbling brook as it leaps with joy down the mountain side into the valley to bring light and happiness to every little blade and petal, until the barren vale is made to revive the songs of Eden … Why, after I have considered the lilies in all their beauty, I become so inspired that I lift my eyes and gaze into the heavens at the stars and like the shepherds, who saw the Star hanging over Bethlehem and were guided by its brightness to the manger, to the swaddling-clothed babe, wrapped in

> its kingly innocence, lying in a golden manger, I am
> swept into ethereal spheres where I am bathed with the
> effulgent glory of the Eternal God of Ages … Amen.

And then he would cast aside the trappings of make-believe and launch into his edgy word regarding sin and repentance, leading to salvation. The point was not to stir the listeners to a sort of 'jihad,' reminiscent of Pope Urban's call to attack the Saracens, but rather to self-examination, whereby people became broken-hearted over the wreckage they'd made of their lives; of their indifference to the needs of their neighbors, spiritual and temporal; and of their need to minister to them, not at the point of a sword, but with a cup of cold water. If there's a holy war, it's declared on their own selfishness, and the listeners don't come charging out of the church to attack the infidel as much as to serve him or her in Jesus' name, which may well include persuading the non-believer (and not coercing) away from their self-destructive ways.

Of course, preaching is the focus of the Awakenings, whether from George Whitefield, John Wesley, Billy Sunday, or Mordecai Ham. But music plays a powerful role in the movement of the Spirit. William Rees's song, 'Here is Love' (1900), was a hallmark of and impetus for the Welsh revival. It pictures the inrushing of redeeming grace that addresses the toxins of sin:

On the mount of crucifixion,
Fountains opened deep and wide;
Through the floodgates of God's mercy
Flowed a vast and gracious tide.
Grace and love, like mighty rivers,
Poured incessant from above,
And heav'n's peace and perfect justice
Kissed a guilty world in love.

Then there were the Billy Graham Crusades, 417 of them in 185 countries/territories, with 215 million in attendance, and 2.2 million decisions recorded in response to the invitations, which were typically offered over the music of 'Just as I Am', written by Charlotte Elliott in 1835:

Just as I am – without one plea,
But that Thy blood was shed for me,
And that Thou bidst me come to Thee,
– O Lamb of God, I come! …

Just as I am – though toss'd about
With many a conflict, many a doubt,
Fightings and fears within, without,
– O Lamb of God, I come!

Just as I am – poor, wretched, blind;
Sight, riches, healing of the mind,
Yea, all I need, in Thee to find,
– O Lamb of God, I come! …

Graham also drew frequently on Stuart Hine's 1949 translation of Carl Gustav Boberg's 'How Great Thou Art' (sung by George Beverly Shea before the message):

> … And when I think that God, His Son not sparing,
> Sent Him to die, I scarce can take it in;
> That on the cross, my burden gladly bearing,
> He bled and died to take away my sin.
>
> Then sings my soul, my Savior God, to Thee;
> How great Thou art …

EDUCATIONAL INSTITUTIONS

For centuries, Christian colleges and universities have been accountability agents for the Church. Alongside the ministry of Bible schools and seminaries, Liberal Arts colleges have addressed and advanced the disciplines of mathematics and the natural sciences (biology, physics, astronomy, geology), of the social sciences (anthropology, economics, geography, history, jurisprudence, linguistics, political science and sociology), of the arts (painting and sculpture, music, drama and literature), and of other classical studies in philosophy, rhetoric and logic. It makes for an energizing interplay of ideas, summoning critical tools to the fore.

Recognizing the value of this enterprise, virtually all faith groups have established such schools. I think, for instance, of the athletic conference in which Wheaton (the college

I served in the 1970s) competed. The College Conference of Illinois and Wisconsin (CCIW) was composed of our non-denominational school, plus Illinois Wesleyan (United Methodist), Augustana (Scandinavian Evangelical Lutheran), North Park (Swedish Evangelical Lutheran), North Central (United Methodist), Elmhurst (German Evangelical Synod/United Church of Christ), Millikin (Presbyterian) and Carroll (Presbyterian).

Founded as Christian institutions, they honored doctrinal boundaries, but, within those limits, articulate and even contentious voices spoke to the virtues and foibles, the insights, blind spots and confusions of the family of God. One aesthetician would argue that modern art was deplorable, while another would find much value in it; one sociologist would hail the election of a 'progressive' politician, while another would campaign for his 'conservative' opponent; one biologist would champion 'young earth' creationism, while another would take the 'old earth' position. And the debate has ranged beyond particular departments and faculties to conferences and periodicals. It has been—and continues to be—a lively tradition, one in which boneheaded insularity and manipulative indoctrination can scarcely prosper.

While some schools put more stress upon the classroom than upon publish-or-perish scholarship, Christian professors do, indeed, publish a great deal, weighing in on every issue from global warming to tax rates, from civil liberties to existentialism. In all this, they seek to 'integrate faith and learning,' with much of that learning coming from universities outside their faith tradition—with Presbyterians earning PhDs from Notre Dame, Baptists from Harvard and Methodists from UCLA.

Through the centuries, Christians have been trailblazing academics of the highest order, setting the pace worldwide for founding institutions of academic honor, from the Sorbonne to Oxford to Princeton. And the educational impulse is not limited to one denomination or another, but is an outworking of scholarly seriousness wherever the Bible is in play. In this connection, Christian ethicists, whether or not in denominational employ, have brought prophetic and convicting words to bear on abuses inflicted in the name of God. For instance, Francisco de Vitoria, founder of the Catholic 'School of Salamanca,' harshly criticized Spain's brutal treatment (with church co-operation) of indigenous people in the New World, writing such words as, 'The conclusion of all that has been said is that the barbarians undoubtedly possessed as true dominion, both public and private, as any Christians' and 'It may be asked ... whether Christian princes can convert them by violence and the sword ... ? The reply is that they cannot, because the king of Spain has no greater power over them than I do over my fellow citizens; but I cannot compel a fellow citizen to hear mass; *ergo*.'[5]

Christian scholars keep an eye on the Church. Meanwhile, the Church keeps an eye on its scholars, and sometimes, with warrant, moves to defund or rework schools abandoning their early doctrinal commitments. But accountability comes from outside as well, in that Christian colleges and universities typically seek accreditation, whereby they're answerable to secular authorities, who insist, for instance, that the professors' degrees come from a variety of sound universities lest faculties become 'inbred.' Of course, the accreditors themselves can be obsessed with bureaucratic minutiae and may well have some ideological bias, but Christian schools have managed to carve out a respectable, even, at times, splendid level of scholarship, according to accreditors.

CHRISTIAN BOOK PUBLISHING

Though much could be said for the salutary effect of the electronic media in Christian hands—radio, television, online periodicals, podcasts, and such—let me focus rather on this venerable medium, the book. Yes, there are wonderful print magazines and papers as well, powerful antibodies, doing their cleansing work by highlighting inspirational

5   Francisco de Vitoria, *Political Writings*, edited by Anthony Pagden and Jeremy Lawrence (Cambridge: Cambridge University Press, 1991), 250, 346.

deeds, by adjudicating 'family' disputes, by doing the tough work of investigative journalism, by rallying the troops for social action, and by walking us out of fever swamps of confusion—a too brief a word of appreciation, but let's press on.

Christian publishing houses supply the faithful with books covering a wide range of topics, from biblical studies to apologetics to Church history to personal finances to theology to cultural engagement: dozens of topics. And not a few are directed toward cleaning up the moral act of the faithful, either as individuals or within congregations. A classic in this genre is Carl F. H. Henry's *The Uneasy Conscience of Fundamentalism,* wherein he observed, 'The Great Majority of Fundamentalist clergymen, during the past generation of world disintegration, became increasingly less vocal about social evils.'[6]

In this vein, Emmanuel Kampouris (the retired CEO of American Standard Corporation) and his wife Camille published a website (kairosjournal.org) designed to encourage and equip pastors to engage the culture prophetically on a broad range of topics. They did so in response to the lethargy they observed in the political arena, and they were inspired by the examples of both Clapham pastor, John Venn, (who was an encouragement to William Wilberforce during the

---

6   Carl F. H. Henry, *The Uneasy Conscience of Modern Fundamentalism* (Grand Rapids: Eerdmans, 1947), 4.

years he was crusading for the abolition of slavery in the British Empire) and Pastor André Trocmé (who led his little congregation to hide Jews from the authorities in Vichy France).

In due course, hundreds of these articles were selected for the *NKJV Unapologetic Study Bible*. For instance, 'The *Haggadot* Distraction' draws upon Paul's warning, in 1 Timothy 1, against 'fables and endless genealogies' and 'stories that gave rise to Pharisaical regulations.' In modern terms, church leaders can develop their own *haggadot*:

> [I]ntricately constructed codes for Christian 'righteousness' based upon anecdotal evidence rather than Bible power. Men arrogantly constructed the new 'laws' that detail 'acceptable' Christian behavior down to the minutest detail, whether in the realm of courtship, the choice of Bible translations, or the use/ disuse of neckties. This is to trivialize God's great work on the heart, by faith which wells up in righteousness, faithfulness, and obedience.[7]

Thus, Christians speak through a Christian book publisher to Christians, applying the Apostle's writing to the Church.

But Christians can also marshal the writings of non-Christians to admonish their fellow believers. This same study Bible quotes Alan Wolfe, a political science professor

---

7   *NKJV Unapologetic Study Bible: Confidence for Such a Time as This* (Nashville: Thomas Nelson, 2017), 1376.

and avowed agnostic, who had crossed America to visit a variety of churches. In the end, he assured his fellow secularists that Evangelicals posed little threat to the march of their values, for

> They say they believe the Bible is the word of God, but somehow strangely the Bible always says what satisfies their personal psychological and emotional needs. They say they worship an awesome God, but their deity is not one to be feared because he is pretty much nonjudgmental, always quick to point out your good qualities, and will take whatever he can get in terms of your commitment to him. He's 'God lite'—not the imposing deity before whom Israel trembled at the foot of Mt. Sinai, but the sort of deity who is always there to give you fresh supplies of upbeat daily therapy. And as for God's people, well, they are really just like everyone else—no more holy or righteous than the rest of us. Put them in the crucible of character and they'll fold like a cheap suit. In sum, democracy is safe from religious zealots because such people don't really exist in large numbers.[8]

Stinging but needful words. Never mind that they come from a non-believer. For 'all truth is God's truth,' and so is fit for the pages of a Christian publisher's book.

---

8   *Unapologetic Study Bible*, 1471.

EARLY CRITICS FROM WITHIN THE FOLD

In the sixteenth century, Erasmus penned *In Praise of Folly*, mocking church scholars who

> ... labor some theological question which has no relation to anything on earth or in heaven, but which they judge is an important part of their art. Here at last, they reach the theological heights, drumming into the ears of the audience those imposing titles: Illustrious Doctor, Subtle Doctor, Super-subtle Doctor, Seraphic Doctor, Holy Doctor, Invincible Doctor. Before the simple people, they toss back and forth their syllogisms, majors, minors, conclusions, corollaries, conversions—all the lifeless and more than scholastic pedantry.[9]

And he did not spare the Pope:

> Finally, if the Supreme Pontiffs, who are the vicars of Christ, tried to imitate His life, His poverty, labors, teachings, His cross and contempt for life; if they stopped to consider the meaning of the title Pope, a Father, or the epithet Most Holy, who on earth would be more overwhelmed? Who would purchase that office at the cost of every effort? Who would retain it by the sword, by poison, and by every other way? If wisdom should come to Popes, what comforts it would deprive them of! Did I say wisdom? Even that grain of sense which Christ speaks of would do it. It would

---

9   Desiderius Erasmus, 'The Praise of Folly,' translated by Leonard F. Dean, *Essential Works of Erasmus*, edited by W.T.H. Jackson (New York: Bantam, 1965), 412-413.

deprive them of all wealth, honor, and possessions; all the triumphal progresses, office, dispensations, tributes, and indulgences; the many horses, mules, and retainers; in short, it would deprive them of all their pleasures.[10]

In the seventeenth century, French philosopher, Blaise Pascal, raised his voice in *Provincial Letters*, indicting the Jesuits for their 'casuistry,' (their use of clever but unsound reasoning in relation to moral questions) through which counsel they were able to give miscreants an easy, clean bill of health. This proved particularly useful with regard to the Roman Catholic sacrament of penance, whereby priests would hear confessions and assess penalties to restore one's righteousness and maintain their hope of heaven.

The word 'casuistry' is not itself condemnatory, for it simply means applying principles to tough cases drawing on the counsel of earlier, similar cases—precedents—the sort of thinking employed in English Common Law decisions. The problem comes (and came in Pascal's day) when you introduce a range of clever loopholes to accommodate the sins of counselees. This was the sort of thing Pascal saw in play, and he named names as he identified those who were working the religious scam.

---

10   Erasmus, 416-417.

One was a Monsieur le Moine, a Sorbonne professor representing the views of Cardinal Richelieu.[11] He argued that, for something to count as a sin, the one who did the act must have done so with knowledge of his moral problem, knowledge of the Lord's spiritual solution, a desire to be healed of his moral sickness, and a desire to pray for divine help. If, though, he pressed ahead in his actions, it would count as a transgression. Of course, Pascal found this absurd. It would imply that an enthusiastic gang of thugs were as pure as the driven snow since they were innocent in their ignorance and willfulness. They simply couldn't help themselves, so we must not judge them harshly as they carry out their various robberies, assaults, and chicaneries.

Pascal was just getting warmed up when he went after a Father Bauney, who was touting the principle of 'probabilism,' which taught that it was enough to find just one educated authority who agreed with you to escape judgment for some widely-condemned practice you'd adopted. (In this, Bauney followed the thinking of 'celebrated casuist, Basil Ponce.') This authority's opinion didn't have to be knock-down certain, but only more or less probable, the same as was true for all opinions. So you were free to take your pick, never mind that the one you'd chosen

11 Blaise Pascal, 'The Provincial Letters,' IV and V, in *Great Books of the Western World*, vol. 33, edited by Robert Maynard Hutchins (Chicago: Encyclopedia Britannica, 1952), 19-35.

was wildly implausible and almost universally rejected. If you could find an academic to make out your case, then you could 'claim sanctuary' and avoid rebuke.

Of course, anyone familiar with the world of scholars knows that you can *always* find some curiosity on some faculty or other to be your ideological or ethical friend. In our day, for instance, Princeton philosopher Peter Singer has shown some support for bestiality, and Northwestern University electrical engineering professor Arthur Butz has become notorious as a Holocaust denier. Both present arguments for their position, so, on Father Bauney's model, both men offer moral refuge for their followers.

Yes, there is a difference in that those who followed the principle of probabilism of Pascal's day were dealing with those professing allegiance to the Bible, but the peril extends to the secular academy. Both camps can accommodate the breezy dismissal of strong ethical counsel, and both can hand out excuses to those who need firm moral correction.

FINANCIAL ACCOUNTABILITY

I recently turned through a copy of my denominational state paper and found that several pages were given over to a minute listing of each church's offering to missions' causes beyond its doors. This is commonplace in our particular tribe, and, for years, I thought it was a means of both acclaim and shame, a tool of peer pressure. After all, who wants to be widely known as miserly? But I learned that there was another important function: financial accountability. Since the papers went to clergy and laity alike, everyone was invited to check out their own church's record, and sometimes there are shocks. 'Wait! I thought we gave at least $500 to the Christmas offering for international missions. This has us giving nothing. What's going on?' And so we check with the pastor or treasurer to see what happened to that designated money. In the vast majority of cases, there's a simple, acceptable explanation ('We were waiting for that last, promised check before sending in the sum.') But sometimes, it's a matter of negligence ('Sorry, but I was studying for my realtor's license, and I got behind.') or of understandable but unacceptable finagling ('We had to draw on this fund to pay the quarterly insurance premium, but we'll replenish it and send the money along. Just a timing difference.') Sad to say, these lists have outed real thieves from time to time, people who've been diverting funds into their own accounts.

Parachurch groups are also susceptible to this sort of sin, so, in 1979, a number of them founded the Evangelical Council for Financial Accountability (ECFA at ecfa.org), dedicated to 'enhancing trust in Christ-Centered Churches and Ministries.' They operated with Seven Standards of Responsible Stewardship, including effective board oversight, transparency in communication, responsible compensation-setting, and fidelity to donor intent. Thus, they sought to establish their own version of the Better Business Bureau, Consumer Reports, or the Good Housekeeping Seal.

Though ECFA has done some good work through the years, yet another parachurch organization, WORLD News Group (through their magazine *WORLD*), ran an article in 2019 saying the ECFA was guilty of 'grade inflation,' letting some less-than-circumspect people off the hook, giving them 'an easy A.'[12] But again, this is an example of how watchdogs watch the watchdogs in the world of Christian accountability.

DECLARATIONS

Christians also correct themselves through declarations when they find their moral house is in disorder. However, we don't speak monolithically. For instance, we've differed for centuries over the morality of war, capital punishment, and standards for divorce and remarriage. Typically, the dispute centers on Scripture interpretation, with, for instance, pacifists pointing to John 18:11, where Jesus told Peter to sheathe his sword, and just-war advocates quoting Romans 13:1-7 to justify the state's use of deadly force. In other instances, it's a dispute over the facts of the matter.

Take the issue of human-induced global warming. The Evangelical Climate Initiative issued 'Climate Change:

---

12 Michael Reneau, 'An easy "A,"' *WORLD* (September 12, 2018). Accessed January 6, 2020 at https://world.wng.org/2019/09/an_easy_a.

An Evangelical Call to Action,' wherein they insisted that we must 'begin to reduce the carbon dioxide emissions from the burning of fossil fuels' lest 'millions of people … die in this century … most of them our poorest global neighbors.' In response, the Cornwall Alliance published 'An Evangelical Declaration on Global Warming,' claiming that, as a result of God's design and power, 'Earth and its ecosystems … are robust, resilient, self-regulating, and self-correcting …' They are not 'the fragile and unstable products of chance,' and whatever recent warming there might be is 'neither abnormally large nor abnormally rapid.' In an ancillary document, 'A Renewed Call to Truth, Prudence, and Protection of the Poor,' they said that 'global warming alarmism' came up short in 'theology, science, and economics.'

Yes, 'good people disagree,' but the language of dispute over this matter is not always so charitable. When 'destruction of the planet' or 'pointless destruction of the means of progress' are the notions in play, one's opponent can quickly become anathema. Nevertheless, Christians can help show each other the way out of whatever muddle or madness they might have suffered, for, as it says in 1 Corinthians 13:6, 'love … rejoices with the truth.' This may sound like a sweet platitude in this context, but it can make all the difference. In a world more concerned with pride, power and wealth than love, it is very difficult for many to not only admit that

163

they are wrong or that their opponent has a good point, but also to celebrate the revelation with something like, 'I'm so grateful to you for helping me sort things out. What a relief. Thank you so much. I may have lost some of my caché as a thinker and advocate, but no one wants to be celebrated for the wrong thing.'

Far-fetched? Not when the Spirit of Christ reigns in the Body.

SUMMARY OF MAIN POINTS

- Congregations, communities and nations can be reformed by revivals and awakenings.
- Educational institutions, a mainstay of Christian culture, provide correction and direction.
- Christian publishing is free and wide-ranging in its moral impact.
- Church history is replete with dissident voices who have worked to keep us honest.
- Issue-oriented parachurch groups also hold the church accountable, whether through financial reports or public policy declarations.

11

Environmental Protection

As powerfully beneficial as antibodies are to health, it is foolish to put them to the test by careless attention to healthful practices and cleanliness. Wash your hands. Brush your teeth. Keep food that can spoil refrigerated. And, of course, be considerate of the environment you share with others. Sneeze or cough into your elbow. And so on.

So what's the application to this book? Well, it's not a license for cleansing the public square of unholy things, of temptations that might corrupt Christians. It's not a call for stifling hostile voices. The authorities tried that in Massachusetts Bay Colony (and Mecca for that matter). On the contrary, I'm urging a free marketplace of ideas, where the germs of folly are given their space in social discourse.

Notwithstanding the COVID discussion of recent years, an analogy suggests itself. It's often say that kids are more susceptible to germs because they've been so sheltered from them, deprived of the chance to build up antibodies. Splashed with hand sanitizers at every turn, they live in a germ-free utopia, which serves them poorly down the line. The classic essayist Montaigne said that we must all eat our 'barrel of dirt' in life—not all at once, but cumulatively. He wasn't celebrating this unsavory diet, but there is a 'silver lining' to this phenomenon.

Of course, in the history of the faith, there have been pockets and seasons of Christendom when and where dissenting voices were suppressed. Heretics have been squashed, books burned by authorities and troublemakers banished. But the faithful have come to understand that insularity breeds intolerance, and most have learned by now that outsiders keep us honest.

ROGER WILLIAMS AND JOHN LELAND

The Baptists, with their work for 'a free church in a free state,' deserve a special place of honor in reversing the totalitarian impulses of the Puritans. In *The Bloudy Tenent of Persecution for cause of Conscience, discussed, in a conference between Truth and Peace,* Roger Williams maintained that 'it is the will and command of God, that since the coming of His Son the Lord Jesus, a permission of the most paganish,

Jewish, Turkish, or antichristian consciences and worships, be granted in all nations and countries,' for, in His earthly ministry, Jesus 'never appointed the civil sword for either antidote or remedy' toward those who rejected Him.

Williams was a renegade minister in Puritan Massachusetts Bay Colony. Though Cambridge-trained and initially well-affirmed by men of stature, including the British jurist, Thomas Coke, and colonial governor, William Bradford, he soon found himself at odds with his fellow clergy on a number of matters, including his contempt for the licensure requirement for colonial churches by both the English crown and archbishops; their insistence that the state could punish people for indifference to the first four of the Ten Commandments (no other gods; no idols; God's name in vain; Lord's Day observance); and his high esteem for the colonists' Native American neighbors. So, he was banished from the colony in 1635 and took up residence among the Narragansett Indians in what is today known as Rhode Island.

A century and a half later, officials of a newly-independent America had drafted a Constitution, and ratification by the states was sought. Baptist preacher, John Leland, opposed its current form since he felt it didn't ensure religious liberty. He trusted that such leaders as James Madison, Thomas Jefferson and George Washington were devoted to this freedom, but Leland wasn't confident that these rights would remain secure once these men had passed from the scene. Hearing of his reservations, Madison sought him out and pledged to press for an amendment which would address Leland's fears. Leland threw his support behind Madison and ratification, and, true to his word, Madison led the successful effort to attach a Bill of Rights. The First Amendment, now part of the founding document, read:

> Congress shall make no law respecting an establishment of religion, or prohibiting the free exercise thereof; or abridging the freedom of speech, or of the press; or the right of the people peaceably to assemble, and to petition the Government for a redress of grievances.

Before his death, Leland insisted on a simple service with a grave marker bearing the words, 'Here lies the body of John Leland, who labored 67 years to promote piety, and vindicate the civil and religious rights of all men.'

John Milton

Of course, Williams and Leland were not the first to champion this cause. The Protestant poet, John Milton, was upset that a seventeenth-century Protestant parliament was intent on requiring licensure for publishers—a measure designed to prevent ideological infection by radicals, royalists and other troublemakers. (Indeed, he'd been a troublemaker himself by virtue of his writing in favor of exceptions for divorce and remarriage.) These were the days when Europe, including England, was apt to deploy troops and execute people over religious disagreement (which was essentially political disagreement in most cases), so the act was not so much a protocol for a society-wide debating club as a matter of wartime censorship. Nevertheless, Milton argued that they were making a big mistake, and he marshalled Scripture to make his case. (The name of his tract, *Areopagitica*, derives from Mars Hill in Athens, where Greeks held disputations and trials—Mars being the Roman god of war, Ares his Greek counterpart.)

He began with words from Euripides, 'This is true liberty when free-born men having to advise the public may speak free ....' and then held up as a cautionary example the papal proscription of writings, as in the Inquisition. He cited the Bible generously in making his appeal, noting the 'examples of Moses, Daniel and Paul, who were skillful in all the learning of the Egyptians, Chaldeans and Greeks, which could not probably be without reading their books of all sorts, in Paul especially, who thought it no defilement to insert into holy scripture the sentences of three Greek poets ... '[1]

He spoke to fellow believers, arguing that their best development depended upon conflict:

> I cannot praise a fugitive and cloistered virtue, unexercised and unbreathed, that never sallies out

---

1   John Milton, *Areopagitica and Other Writings*, edited by William Poole (London: Penguin, 2014), 108.

> and sees her adversary, but slinks out of the race ... Assuredly we bring not innocence into the world, we bring impurity much rather: that which purifies us is trial, and trial is by what is contrary. That virtue therefore which is but a youngling in the contemplation of evil, and knows not the utmost that vice promises to her followers, and rejects it, is but a blank virtue ....[2]

Though Parliament went ahead to enact the law, Milton's piece has become a classic in Western thought, with a portion displayed over the entrance to the reading room at the New York Public Library and with citation in a variety of U.S. Supreme Court cases defending broad freedom of speech, including that of contraception advocates and Communists when their perspectives were counted particularly onerous.

BASIL OF CAESAREA

Turning back to the fourth century, we find these words from 'Saint Basil the Great,' a champion of orthodoxy through the Nicene Creed. Here he urges forbearance and charity in our dealings with enemies of the faith:

> [L]et's take on board everything in Pagan literature that encourages us to pursue worthwhile things. We also have the virtuous deeds of Pagans, either documented in history, in accounts passed down in unbroken tradition, or set down on paper by poets or writers of prose. The example of these virtuous deeds should also edify us. For instance, there was a fellow hanging about

---

2   *Areopagitica*, 111.

in the town centre of Athens who kept heaping abuse on Pericles, but Pericles turned a deaf ear. The fellow kept it up all day long, plastering Pericles with vicious insults. Still Pericles took no notice. When evening fell and it got dark, the fellow was still raging away. Yet Pericles chaperoned him home with a lamp! You see, Pericles didn't want his own training in philosophy to be meaningless.[3]

In contemporary times, the helpfulness of unmuzzled atheists is manifest. Consider

- Upton Sinclair's *The Jungle*, which helped bring reform to the meat-packing industry, both with regard to cruelty to animals and hygiene.
- Linus Pauling, winner of the Nobel Prize in chemistry, whose work paved the way for understanding DNA.
- Richard Rogers, whose musical scores for such shows as *Oklahoma*, *The King and I* and *The Sound of Music* delighted audiences.
- Oliver Sacks, a neurologist who chronicled groundbreaking work in *Awakenings*.
- Steve Wozniak, who co-founded Apple.

It's ironic that while Christians have forged space for 'nones' (those professing no religion) to speak freely, the secular university campuses, where nones abound, are no longer

---

3   St. Basil of Caesarea, quoted in *Daily Readings: The Early Church Fathers*, edited by Nick Needham (Tain, Ross-shire: Christian Heritage/Christian Focus, 2017), May 26.

bastions of free speech, but rather they obsesses over 'safe spaces' where 'snowflake' students can be protected from people and views they find upsetting. Ironically, the secular academy is using the liberty that biblical Christians help provide it to turn around and curb the liberty of their Christian students (especially Evangelicals) to express themselves biblically and freely. (Just yesterday, I heard the recollection of a student who was reprimanded for inviting men on his dorm floor to a Bible study. When 'called on the carpet,' he asked the dean of students if that meant it was fine to ask people down the hall to a keg party but not to a session on Scripture. The blunt answer was Yes. And this at a school founded by Methodists.)

BUCHAREST

In the early 1990s, I traveled to Bucharest with a group of eight from our denomination. We were there not long after the deposition of Ceaușescu, and the nation was trying to set itself aright. Under the Communist tyrant, all Christian churches (Evangelical, Catholic and Orthodox) were more or less oppressed, suppressed and persecuted. (I was told that a favorite method of murdering troublesome pastors was through staged traffic accidents where big trucks would slam into their cars from the side.) It was a matter of sweet justice that the spark which had ignited the revolution was struck in Timisoara, at the spot where the state was tormenting a Reformed pastor.

One would think, then, that the new day would see religious liberty for all, but the Romanian Orthodox Church was arrogating to itself special status, with exclusive prerogatives it enjoyed before the Communists took control after World War II. On this model, the Evangelicals and Catholics were again being mistreated, though, of course, not as harshly. But we hoped to point to a better way, so we scheduled meetings with parliamentarians and government officials, seeking to persuade them that the First Amendment to the U.S. Constitution, with its establishment and free exercise clauses, was salutary.

I was assigned to speak on the secular advantages of such a policy, and I noted that countries which encouraged the free exchange of ideas, which esteemed and protected generous input from all sorts of people, were most likely to develop great universities, enjoy the productive research and development of new inventions, and find themselves honored and emulated among nations.

DAVID BARROW AND ROBERT BARNES

Of course, many struggles for liberty are waged against powers hostile to Christianity, whether Kim Jong-un or the Taliban, but churchgoers have often had to lock horns with other churchgoers to set things right, not only within the church, but also throughout society. In this connection, it's surprising how hermeneutics can impact the public square.

Take the case of Ham. When the heroic Noah disgraced himself, post flood, by making a drunken spectacle of himself, he pronounced a curse on a whole race of men. One of his sons, Ham, found him lying naked and inebriated in his tent and ran to tell his brothers, Shem and Japheth. They refused to witness the debacle, but rather backed into the tent with a covering garment, averting their eyes. Noah appreciated their gracious care, but was incensed at Ham's behavior, unloading on him, saying that Ham's son, Canaan, would suffer servitude at the hands of his brother's people (Gen. 9:20-27).

Somehow, this came to be interpreted as a standing judgment on black people, so that, throughout history, they should be subjugated by Europeans (from Japheth) and Semitic groups (from Shem). Quite an interpretive leap, but quite convenient for those who wanted to mistreat Africans. All sorts of people got in on the act, including Gulliaume-Rene Meignan, Catholic Archbishop of Tours, who, in 1869, traced the 'unfortunate' and 'abased' condition of the 'black race' to the 'curse pronounced against Canaan'; Baptist clergyman, John Dagg, who, in 1859, said that American slaves should 'submit patiently to the curse which has doomed them to bondage'; Methodist minister, John Bell Robinson, who said, in 1863, that 'there would have been no slaves nor negroes in this world of ours' if Ham had been true to his father; Presbyterian theologian, Robert Dabney, who, in 1867, said that this 'biblical text provided divine sanction for the enslavement of blacks'; Episcopal bishop, George Freeman, who, in 1837, said that the 'present degraded condition is a manifest fulfillment' of the curse.

But this opinion would not stand, for it was met with counter-arguments from the same ranks of the clergy, the majority of whom said that such application was an abomination. For instance, in 1802, Kentucky Baptist pastor, David Barrow, declared, 'I am persuaded, that no passage in the sacred volume of Revelation, has suffered more abuse, than "Noah's curse or malediction" as it is generally expressed by friends of despotism …' In 1846, Philadelphia Presbyterian minister, Albert Barnes, echoed his sentiment: 'This passage, by a singular perverseness of interpretation, and a singular perseverance in that perverseness notwithstanding the plainest rules of exegesis, is often employed to justify the reduction of the African to slavery …'[4]

Inevitably, this latter group prevailed, for the slavery-friendly reading was unsustainable. Furthermore, the curse-deniers had the force of arms on their side, and Northern Baptists, Presbyterians, Methodists, Anglicans and others

---

4   These voices found in David M. Goldenberg, *Black and Slave: The Origins and History of the Curse of Ham* (Berlin/Boston: DeGruyter, 2017), 119-120, 216.

were able to enforce a more godly interpretation on their southern counterparts in the church. Thus, they sang, in 'The Battle Hymn of the Republic',

> Mine eyes have seen the glory of the coming of the Lord,
> He is trampling out the vintage where the grapes of wrath are stored,
> He hath loosed the fateful lightning of his terrible swift sword,
> His truth is marching on.

JERRY MITCHELL

In June of 1964, one of the most deplorable events in American history took place in Neshoba County, Mississippi. Three civil rights workers, James Chaney, Andrew Goodwin and Michael Schwerner, were murdered by a gang of ten, commissioned by the Ku Klux Klan. Among them was Edgar Ray 'Preacher' Killen, a part-time minister. (He was released after the initial trial, with the jury deadlocked at 11-1, the lone holdout saying she couldn't vote to convict a preacher. Later, the case was reopened, and he went to jail, where he died at age ninety-two.)

Jerry Mitchell, who also professed faith in Christ, was instrumental in bringing Killen to justice. As the account goes:

> In the long run, a new generation of political leaders, prosecutors, and activists have come of age determined

to overturn the wrongs of the past. One of those leaders is the journalist Jerry Mitchell, whom the *Atlanta Constitution* dubbed a 'red-headed, Southern fried Colombo.' After graduating from college Mitchell started working at small newspapers in Texas and Arkansas. Motivated by a deep Christian faith and a strong sense of social justice, he decided to turn his investigative skills to investigate civil rights. 'It says in Psalms, "God loves justice,"' he said. 'It's a part of who we Christians are. I don't think God ever intended for someone to walk away from a murder.'[5]

Sometimes, Christians have to run their own brethren to ground to ensure that the environment for those outside the fold are protected, including Schwerner and Goodman, who were Jewish.

John Calvin

Though John Calvin's Geneva was not a bastion of religious freedom, having infamously executed the heretic, Servetus, we can thank Calvin for his theological efforts in advancing the doctrine of the depravity of man. This tenet of the faith played in the mind of many in the colonies, including that of Presbyterian pastor, John Witherspoon, the only clergyman to sign the Declaration of Independence. Convinced that humanity was not basically good or worthy of unqualified trust, the founders built many checks and balances into the

---

5   Steven M. Gillon, *10 Days that Unexpectedly Changed America* (New York: Broadway, 2006), 250-251.

Constitution and provided the path to other limits on power to be added through amendment. And thus we have the separation of powers among the legislative, executive and judicial branches; term limits; vetoes and veto overrides; and impeachments. The Catholic Lord Acton is known for his resonance with this sentiment, having said, 'Power tends to corrupt and absolute power corrupts absolutely.'

PETER MARSHALL

A native Scotsman, Peter Marshall, became pastor of New York Avenue Presbyterian Church, Washington, D.C. in 1937, and, in 1947, he began serving as Chaplain of the U.S. Senate, a position he held until his untimely death in 1949 at age forty-six. His was an extraordinary life, captured in biography, *A Man Called Peter*, by his wife, Catherine, a story made into an Oscar-nominated film of the same name.

Though absolute church-state separationists object to the very notion of a Senate Chaplain, they ignore the Constitutional vision of the nation's Founders, who proscribed a national church in the First Amendment's 'establishment clause,' but did not thereby prescribe government devoid of respect for the God of the Bible. And so, this man of the cloth was invited to invoke God's wisdom (and His blessing upon those who honored it) as he 'spoke truth to power' in the halls of Congress. By all accounts, his words were effective deeds of 'environmental protection,' helping to raise the moral tone of the proceedings and the nation at large.

Here's one from March 18, 1947. In it, you can hear an echo of Psalm 51:

> OUR FATHER IN HEAVEN, who dost know every secret of our hearts—all that we fear, all that we hope, and all of which we are ashamed—in this moment of confession, as each man looks into his own heart and mind, have mercy upon us all, and make us clean inside, that in all we do today we may behave with true courtesy and honor. Compel us to be just and honest in all our dealings. Let our motives be above suspicion. Let our word be our bond. Let us be kind in our criticism of others, and slow to judge, knowing that we ourselves must one day be judged. We pray for a new spirit to come upon us that we may be able to do more and better work. Through Jesus Christ our Lord. Amen.[6]

And another on June 13 of that year:

> GOD OF OUR FATHERS, in whose name this Republic was born, we pray that by Thy help we may be worthy to receive Thy blessings upon our labors. In the trouble and uneasy travail before the birth of lasting peace, when men have made deceit a habit, lying an art, and cruelty a science, help us to show the moral superiority of the way of life we cherish. Here may men see truth upheld, honesty loved, and

---

6   Peter Marshall, *The Senate Prayers of Peter Marshall* (Sandwich, Massachusetts: Chapman Billies, 1996), 20-21.

kindness practiced. In our dealing with each other, may we be gentle, understanding, and kind, with our tempers under control. In our dealings with other nations, may we be firm without obstinacy, generous without extravagance, and right without compromise. We do not pray that other nations may love us, but that they may know that we stand for what is right, unafraid, with the courage of our convictions. May our private lives and our public actions be consistent with our prayers. Through Jesus Christ our Lord. Amen.[7]

SUMMARY OF MAIN POINTS

- Religious liberty and freedom of the press, both advanced by Christians, provide non-believers with the power to sort things out for themselves and to criticize the faithful. Without these prerogatives, the flourishing of society is stunted.

- Christians have also used this liberty of expression to rebuke and instruct fellow-believers whose convictions and actions have undermined the common good.

- A range of historical luminaries, including Basil of Caesarea, John Milton and Roger Williams, have strengthened the hand of the Church's critics to keep us honest.

---

7   Marshall, 42-43.

12

The Rest of the Story

At one level, the one on which we've been working, this book's theme question is a pressing one. But at a deeper level, at the heart of the gospel, the issue finally evaporates in astonishing fashion. For, in the ultimate assessment, Christians aren't bad. Rather, they are perfect. Not by their own performance, but by the performance of their Savior, Jesus, who died on the cross to cleanse them from their sins. Their record of misdeeds is expunged and the righteousness of Jesus is credited to them, should they repent of sin and turn to Him in faith. It's pure grace.

The Bible teaches this in a variety of passages, including Isaiah 61:10 ('I delight greatly in the LORD: my soul rejoices in my God. For he has clothed me with garments of salvation and arrayed me in a robe of his righteousness, as a bridegroom adorns his head like a priest, and as a bride adorns herself with her jewels') and 1 John 1:9 ('If we confess our sins, he is faithful and just and will forgive us our sins and purify us from all unrighteousness').

Thus, we sing about it in the hymn, 'My Hope is Built,' by Edward Mote:

> When He shall come with trumpet sound,
> Oh, may I then in Him be found;
> In Him, my righteousness, alone,
> Faultless to stand before the throne.

Again, there's no denying that we Christians do deplorable things and are justly judged when we act dishonorably. And, as individuals, we don't have to search for outside examples to confirm this point. We need only to review our own record of behavior to feel shame. So how might we stand 'faultless … before the throne'? The same way that a delinquent college student, who has run up huge credit card bills, turns tearfully to his forgiving father to pay them off. The child may appear to be ruined financially, but is, in fact, debt free. It's something of an optical illusion, if you will. Though a misdeed may appear to be damnable, in the Christian's case, it is not so, for salvation comes by grace through faith and not through a perfect record of righteous action.

How Do You Like Me Now?

I hope you'll excuse me, a resident of Nashville, for referencing a country music song. Granted, Toby Keith's 'How Do You

Like Me Now?' is sub-Christian, beset with *Schadenfreude*, but there is salvageable application to the issue at hand. The song begins with his recollection of the callous indifference a high school beauty showed him in their student days and then traces their life paths since then, his to the stage and stardom. Keith sings:

> How do you like me now
> Now that I'm on my way
> Do you still think I'm crazy standing here today
> I couldn't make you love me
> But I always dreamed about living in your radio
> How do you like me now?!

Again, Keith's bitter triumphalism is a far cry from Christian grace, but there is a powerful truth of Christianity embedded in the tale. As uninspiring and even repellant as we Christians may be to the skeptics (who've put their trust in someone or something other than Jesus), a day is coming when we will finally be freed of the deleterious and ruinous impact of 'the world, the flesh and the devil.' Our time of more or less disappointing performance here on earth is only an instant compared to our eternal life in heaven, where we will no longer stoop to sin, gripe over reversals, scheme to escape deserved misfortune and succumb to the lies of the great deluder, Satan. We're going to be likeable and thoughtful.

Meanwhile, those who 'married into' material prosperity, academic or philanthropic acclaim, celebrity status, physical pleasure, ideological zeal, or political power are suffering in hell, following their hellish soul sufferings on earth. (I know you're not supposed to mention that in an apologetics book, but we apologists have to be very careful about hedging or hiding our biblical convictions to ingratiate ourselves to the gainsayers or to tender consciences. As one of my colleagues observed, 'Apologetics is the shortest route to heresy I've seen.' And, as Will Metzger argues in his book on evangelism, *Tell the Truth*,[1] those being saved will savor orthodox doctrine as it's laid out before them.)

So, for the balance of their lives (the post-mortem part), Christians aren't 'so bad.' Still, genuine Christians, the truly redeemed, should also exhibit intimations on earth of their glorious life to come.

BAD DAY ON THE RIVERBOAT

Let's note a difference between the high school girl in Toby Keith's song and the skeptic who rejects the faith of bad Christians on earth. The girl, now a woman, can see clearly that Toby amounted to something impressive and that his circumstances are desirable. She may well come round to the judgment that she made a mistake in her earlier assessment. But it's not clear that non-believers would ever be satisfied with the lifestyle of saints, whether on earth or in heaven.

---

1   Will Metzger, *Tell the Truth: The Whole Gospel to the Whole Person by Whole People: A Training Manual on the Message and Methods of God-centered Witnessing* (Downers Grove: InterVarsity, 1984).

In connection, the story is told, sometimes in sermons, of a gambler who, on his way to the waterfront, looked forward to a day of profiting from passengers on a riverboat about to disembark. To his dismay, the boat was pulling away from the dock as he arrived, and, in a feat of desperation, he flung himself across six feet of water, crashing to the deck. But then, to his mortified surprise, he discovered that this particular boat had been rented by a church for a day cruise, and he found no one to engage him in poker. Furthermore, the passengers were breaking out continually in gospel songs and were listening to various speakers present inspirational talks between times of fellowship over the potluck meal they'd assembled. It was a most miserable day for him. He despised his bad fortune and the happy people around him.

Similarly, it's doubtful that the lost would enthuse over the winsomeness of the redeemed in heaven. It seems unlikely that they would relish their company for long. For one thing, they'd be appalled at their joy, given all the bad things they'd done. The spectacle would strike them as unseemly, what with all the mercy and grace bestowed on such questionable folks. And how could these so-called 'redeemed' people stoop to worship a deity responsible for so much suffering and confusion? It's simply not their cup of tea.

Yes, of course, non-Christians can admire and honor Christians for what they've done for society and for them personally. We've met several of them already; for example, Matthew Parris and Ayaan Hirsi Ali, and there are many others, including believers honored by the Israel Holocaust museum, Yad Vashem, as 'Righteous Among the Nations,' including the Dutchman Casper ten Boom (and his daughter Corrie) and Jane Haining, a Church of Scotland missionary in Budapest. But at the deepest level, those who celebrate and champion the gospel—with its exclusive claims, its insistence upon repentance as a condition for grace and its call for holiness—are strange, if not off-putting, in the eyes of the unredeemed. The New Testament makes this clear in a host of ways, whether through counsel or example.

LOOKING FOR A FEW GOOD MEN AND WOMEN

From 1971 to 1984, the United States Marine Corps fielded a recruiting campaign featuring posters with the words, 'The Marines are looking for a few good men,' and, playing off the words of a familiar Lynn Anderson song, 'We don't promise you a rose garden.' There is a sense in which the Church *is* saying the same thing, and a sense in which it *isn't*.

First, for the 'isn't': 1 Corinthians 1:26-29 (quoted in chapter 9) says that God is pleased to make somebodies out of nobodies, so He doesn't survey the world to discover the 'cream of the crop' for His Church. But there is a big 'is' in this: the Lord will do great things with those (both men and women, of course) who surrender to Him in repentance and gratitude for His forgiveness. And it doesn't take anywhere near a majority of the populace to amount to social salt and light, to arrest rot and shine light into the dark places. In fact, it doesn't take nearly a majority of those who identify with the Church, for it is commonly said that 20 per cent of its members do 80 per cent of the giving and serving: a minority of a minority. But the potential impact of this handful of mature Christians is incalculable. And it may well be that today's critic becomes tomorrow's hero in the faith, one whose skepticism over the whole Christian enterprise gives way to zeal for the honor of Christ and His Church, zeal which redoubles as he or she sees the call to counter the disappointing behavior of his or her spiritual brothers and sisters with exemplary performance on his or her own part.

Make no mistake; it's no rose garden. As Jesus said, in John 15:18-19, 'If the world hates you, keep in mind that it hated me first. If you belonged to the world, it would love you as its own. As it is, you do not belong to the world, but I have chosen you out of the world. That is why the world hates you.' And with that hatred comes a measure of shunning, slander and treachery, not to mention physical abuse in some parts of the world. But it's worth it.

So the Church is a mess? Well, then, join up and make it better.

SUMMARY OF MAIN POINTS

- Christians long for the day when they will be free from the baleful, corrupting influence of the world, the flesh and the devil. Then they will be perfect: for eternity.

- It seems to be clear, from the previous page, that they would not be admired by those who are in and of the world.

- Granting the foibles of the Church, the critic is invited to come to Christ and make things better.

Also available in the *Big Ten* Series…

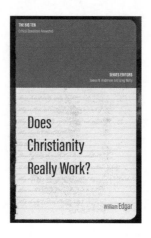

Does Christianity Really Work?

WILLIAM EDGAR

Wasn't the South African Apartheid supported by Christians? Weren't the Crusades motivated by greed, but advocated by the church? Don't phoney television preachers manipulate viewers into donating money? William Edgar addresses these and other questions honestly, without attempting to dismiss or explain away their uncomfortable realities. He displays the good aspects of the church even more brilliantly through frankly and biblically acknowledging the bad. If you have ever asked the question *Does Christianity Really Work?*, this will be an interesting and enlightening read, whatever your prior convictions.

ISBN 978-1-7819-1775-6